CAREER PLANNING
for
BUSINESS
Profiles of Success

Ted Goddard

CONESTOGA COLLEGE

DRYDEN

Harcourt Brace & Company, Canada

TORONTO MONTREAL FORT WORTH NEW YORK ORLANDO
PHILADELPHIA SAN DIEGO LONDON SYDNEY TOKYO

CANADIAN CATALOGUING IN PUBLICATION DATA

Goddard, Ted, 1939–
    Career planning for business.

(Applied business series)
ISBN 0-03-922940-8

1. Business – Vocational guidance. 2. Job hunting – Canada. 3. Career development – Canada. 4. Business students – Employment – Canada. I. Title. II. Series.

HF5382.5.C2G6 1994   650'.023'71   C94-930813-7

Publisher: Heather McWhinney
Editor and Marketing Manager: Donna J. Muirhead
Projects Manager: Liz Radojkovic
Projects Co-ordinator: May Ku
Director of Publishing Services: Jean Davies
Editorial Manager: Marcel Chiera
Production Editor: Louisa Schulz
Production Manager: Sue-Ann Becker
Production Co-ordinator: Carol Tong
Editor: Shirley Tessier
Copy Editor: Jane Lind
Design, Typesetting, and Assembly: ECW Type & Art
Printing and Binding: Best Book Manufacturers, Inc.
Cover image: Tony Stone Images

DRYDEN

This book was printed in Canada on acid-free paper.
1 2 3 4 5   99 98 97 96 95

Table of Contents

ACKNOWLEDGMENTS

Many people helped me prepare this book. As well as the editorial staff at Harcourt Brace, I would like to thank Jean Munro for her help in processing the manuscript; my son Matthew for his research and constructive criticism and my other son Laurence for his contributions to the section on using the computer in the job-search process.

A NOTE
from the
PUBLISHER

Thank you for selecting *Career Planning for Business: Profiles of Success* by Ted Goddard. The author and publisher have devoted considerable time and care to the development of this book. We appreciate your recognition of this effort and accomplishment.

We want to hear what you think about *Career Planning for Business: Profiles of Success*. Please take a few minutes to fill in the stamped reply card at the back of the book. Your comments and suggestions will be valuable to us as we prepare new editions and other books.

*This book is dedicated to all the
students I have had the privilege
of teaching the past 25 years.*

Preface

Every fall, at the conclusion of the baseball season, scores of professional baseball players become free agents. Their career planning consists of looking at the competition's offers, evaluating the organization behind the offer and making their choice. This is a good analogy to career planning for the business students who graduated in the seventies and much of the eighties. Students typically would go to their school's placement office, check the list of companies preparing for on-campus recruiting and sign up for interviews with the ones that sounded interesting. In a few months, these same students would choose from several alternatives the organization and offer that looked best.

Although placement offices on campus continue to play an integral role in career planning for business students, the above strategy does not fit the reality of conditions for students in the nineties. Students who limit their approach to the on-campus recruiters deny themselves an opportunity to have a choice in career options or even to have an offer upon graduation. This book emphasizes the importance of using a multitude of sources and strategies in the job search. Each is discussed in some detail. The relative importance of these sources has changed in recent years and it will, without doubt, continue to change. This book is directed toward business students, but most of the strategies are applicable to students in a postsecondary institution who want some help in planning a career. Should one focus on a specific type of position or use a broader approach and consider general areas of interest?

The book begins with the "how-to" of personal inventory taking — the difficult process of examining yourself. What are your strengths and weaknesses? What do you find interesting; what do you find dull? How might your previous work experience and life experiences have given you skills that are transferable to industry?

The chapters on research and job hunting examine the multitude of sources for discovering what jobs are available and how these sources have changed in the past decade. The preparation of the résumé, and the conflicting views on what constitutes a good résumé, are included. The accompanying covering letter and its important role are also discussed. Many students find the interview the most daunting step in the job-search process. The chapter on interviewing is designed to help you prepare. It covers how to conduct yourself in the interview, the types of questions typically asked, and offers a guide for how you might answer some of the more difficult questions. Other topics in this chapter include interview etiquette and differences between the first and subsequent interviews.

This book concludes with the critical, but often overlooked, strategy of the interview follow-up.

In each chapter, you will find three profiles of recent business graduates who discuss which strategies worked for them in launching their careers.

Career planning is a process. There are logical steps through which all job hunters must go. The book outlines this process in an easy-to-understand, step-by-step sequence. If you follow these steps, you will dramatically increase the odds of getting the job you planned on having after graduation, in the area of your interest.

Career planning, self-assessment, and job-search strategies are as connected as a car's engine is linked to its transmission — one completely relies upon the other. The best job-search strategy without a thorough self-assessment will probably lead either to no job or to an unsuitable one. Good job-search skills accompanied by an excellent résumé might get you an interview, and superior job-interview skills might result in an offer. But three months into the new position as auditor you may feel very unhappy because, for example, of the amount of travel the job demands. The company has branches throughout Canada, and the internal auditor, naturally, has to spend time at each branch. A lack of self-assessment meant that this personal dimension was not considered.

On the other hand, another person's self-assessment might show her or him to be self-directed, with strong analytical skills and a penchant for travelling. Perhaps that person should consider internal auditing as part of their career planning.

In this book, career planning is shown to have two phases. First, based on a self-assessment, what type of career is suitable for you? Second, based on research of the marketplace, what types of career opportunities are emerging? A self-assessment may show someone to be temperamentally suited for a management-trainee position in a large corporation. Researching the marketplace will, however, reveal that that type of position has disappeared. In fact, the same research shows that large corporations will offer a rapidly diminishing share of total graduate placement for at least the balance of this decade.

Most readers will have prepared a s.w.o.t. (strengths, weaknesses, opportunities and threats) analysis for their case studies in a variety of business courses. This is directly analogous to career planning. One has to determine one's strengths and weaknesses, and then marry those to the opportunities and threats in the marketplace.

A frequent question readers ask themselves is "When do I start my career planning?" This is one of the few questions that is easy to answer — start now. If you are in year one of a four-year program, there are steps you can and should take now. In this book we examine strategies you can use in the first year and subsequent years that will give you that "edge" when you enter the competitive phase of active job seeking.

By starting the career-planning process in your first year, you will have identified both your strengths and weaknesses in plenty of time to determine how to further enhance those strengths and, more importantly, overcome your weaknesses. By working through the steps outlined in this book, you may discover that the type of career you are looking for requires skills of which you were unaware. Perhaps many of the recruiters interviewing graduates for industrial accounting positions are looking for people skilled in particular software packages; others recruiting for sales positions want graduates to have a working knowledge of French. If you have identified these requirements well before your graduation year, you will have an opportunity to develop the requisite skills. Many schools offer a broad menu of courses with a relatively small number of required core courses. With such latitude, some of the skills you currently lack may be addressed with available credit courses. In other cases you may take an extra course or two at your school, if available, or at some other educational institution.

A business student I know had a keen interest in working in the pharmaceutical industry. With some basic research, she discovered that pharmaceutical sales staff were primarily science graduates. She had no interest in switching programs, but with a flexible curriculum she was able to take chemistry, biochemistry, and physiology courses. Her long-term career planning impressed two major pharmaceutical companies enough that both offered her a sales position.

A variation on this theme is that if you do your career planning at the beginning of your postsecondary education, you will gain a better appreciation of the importance of the courses you have to take. It is natural for a student to question the relevance of some courses. However, long-term career planning provides incentive to get much more out of a course, because you have an understanding of what skills employers are looking for.

Typically, students understand the importance of their core courses but show less enthusiasm for the peripheral or elective courses. A good understanding of psychology and sociology is important to the marketing student. Economics and statistics are of particular interest to anyone who is considering a career in public service, and business communication courses are critical for everyone who graduates in any business program.

You may be surprised how valuable seemingly irrelevant courses can be. A graduate was recently in a job interview, fully prepared to talk about his strengths, including his work experience and related university courses. The interviewer, a company vice-president, noted that this graduate had taken an elective course in Russian and Chinese political systems and economics. More than half an hour of the interview was taken up with talking about the relative advantages and disadvantages of expanding into each of these countries. The graduate felt comfortable during this discussion but was a bit puzzled at the degree of interest the vice-president showed. As the conversation on this topic concluded, the interviewer revealed that he had just returned from several weeks in Russia and China, as the company was considering expanding operations in those areas. He also indicated surprise at how well-informed the applicant was! The graduate made the next round of interviews and is currently optimistically awaiting word from the company.

CAREER DESIGN SOFTWARE

An exciting inclusion in your copy of *Career Planning for Business: Profiles of Success* is an educational software program especially prepared for students of business.

Created by Eric Sandburg, in collaboration with Crystal-Barkley Corporation, the commercial version of Career Design Software has received rave reviews and recognition in the national press, including *Business Week*, *Fortune*, and *The Wall Street Journal's National Business Employment Weekly*. As a result of the popularity of Career Design Software, Eric Sandburg has been a guest on national radio and television including CNN Business Today, The Larry King/Jim Bohannon Show, and the ABC and CBS networks.

Career design is an ideal supplement to your career planning efforts. It will help you:

- make a personal connection between business topics covered in your program with future careers
- explore what areas of business interest you most
- decide on a major
- discover what career direction you want to pursue
- find out if starting your own business might have a place in your future
- learn your leadership style, and how to improve it
- improve your business and career skills

Career Design Software has been packaged with this book for free. The program requires the use of an IBM compatible PC with 640K RAM.

> If you wish in this world to advance
> Your merits you're bound to enhance;
> You must stir it and stump it,
> And blow your own trumpet,
> Or, trust me, you haven't a chance.
>
> — from *Ruddigore* by W.S. Gilbert

PERSONAL INVENTORY TAKING

 **Profile:** *Tracey L. Stone*

- CURRENT POSITION
  Fund-Raising Coordinator
  Heart and Stroke Foundation of Nova Scotia
  Halifax, Nova Scotia
- EDUCATION
  Bachelor of Commerce, Marketing (Magna Cum
  Laude), 1992, Saint Mary's University

As a result of doing some volunteer work for Heart and Stroke Foundation of Nova Scotia, I was offered a newly formed position with the Heart Foundation and am now time-sharing between the two organizations, although my focus is with the Heart Foundation. My job is to find ways to improve certain programs and to come up with new ones. This can involve researching ideas, watching the competition, looking at past efforts, or meeting with people in the community to see how they would like to benefit from giving a donation or participating in a special event. Fortunately for me, I am able to observe the entire marketing process — ideas go from thought to reality within the organization.

The courses at Saint Mary's dealt mainly with profit organizations, but in my job working for a nonprofit group is different. However, I quickly discovered how to relate what I learned to nonprofit. You are selling something intangible with no fixed price, and there is a *lot* of competition. You also have to be aware of the entire scope of the organization. The bottom line is to raise funds and keep expenses at a minimum, but there is an image to maintain and a public that has to be made aware of what you want to achieve. Results of money earned are hard to come by, since medical research takes time.

My university work and extracurricular activities gave me a pretty good idea of what I was looking for in a future career. Besides taking my classes at Saint Mary's, I worked as a graphic artist for the student government and as a clerk in the university bookstore. I was also involved with the Commerce Society on campus, and held the position of promotions director for one year. Because I worked on so many different things, I quickly learned to manage my time wisely.

I decided early on that I really enjoyed the freedom to use my own judgment. At the bookstore I was allowed to create window displays and rearrange the store. I was asked for my opinion when it came to ordering new merchandise, and was able to keep track of customer comments, both good and bad. I also discovered I preferred to work in a small environment where working relationships took on a personal flavour.

With my preferences in mind, I tailored my courses as I earned my degree. I focused on areas such as promotions and advertising, as I wanted to find out how best to use creative ideas. Projects for these courses involved creating promotional and advertising concepts for companies and determining how such concepts could be best used to benefit what the company wants to achieve. Such practical experience was invaluable. Also, we worked in groups on these projects, and learning how to get the best out of people you may or may not know was a challenge. You get to see how a leader must take charge, delegate, and mediate discussion about the project. It seemed difficult at the time, especially when not everyone would pull their own weight, but this kind of experience prepares you for the workplace.

Working with the Foundation has created a new area of interest for me — computers, especially graphic design. In time, I would like to formally enrol in a graphics design program and eventually find work in this field. I will still aim for small business, as I would like to remain part of the entire development process. If I were to move into the profit sector, I would like to continue my connections with nonprofits, as a volunteer.

◆

▮▮ *Introduction*

"Wanted: A bright, energetic person who has demonstrated leadership skills and works well with people. Strong communication skills, a well-developed sense of organization, and self-direction are essential qualities for anyone applying for this position."

You have seen this statement, or a version of it, in several wanted ads. Perhaps you looked at it and thought, "I'm just an average student who has held only summer and part-time jobs. I don't think I can demonstrate to this company that I have these skills." That is an understandable reaction, but likely incorrect. You have not reached the position of a business student in a postsecondary institution without these and a number of other transferable skills — the skills you have acquired that would be useful in the business world. You are just not aware of who and what you are.

The first step in the job-search process is to determine the answers to some questions about yourself. The result of this self-examination will probably surprise you. The process of answering the question of who and what you are is called "Personal Inventory Taking." This chapter includes a guide on how to prepare your own inventory charts. When you have completed this chapter and have done your own personal inventory, you will have a better idea of your interests, desires, values, and goals.

If you are approaching graduation, you will likely have acquired several years of specialized training, part-time and summer work experience, as well as having participated in extracurricular activities.

"I coached volleyball when I was a senior student at high school." "I helped organize a fund-raising campaign for a charitable cause on campus." "I was cocaptain of the basketball team." "When I worked at the gas bar, I often had to close up and make bank deposits." "I was never viewed as a supervisor when I worked in the clothing store but whenever a new person was hired for my area, I had to help show them the ropes." "When I worked in the accounts department at the store, I often dealt with people on the phone who were pretty upset at some error in their monthly statement."

The student making these statements could be the same one who, in the introduction to this chapter, believed that they were just "average" and not really qualified for the advertised job. Remember those required qualifications of leadership, strong communication skills, a sense of organization, and self-direction? Based on the student's experience, they may indeed have the requisite qualifications. This illustration points out the importance of knowing the product you are going to be marketing — yourself. Keep in mind that this test is only one component of planning your career, and should be used in conjunction with other career-planning activities. Indeed, an unrealistic self-evaluation can lead to a frustrating waste of time competing for jobs for which you are not suited and have little chance of getting, or even to spending much of your life in a job for which you are not well suited.

▌▌ The Self-Assessment Process — Going under the Microscope

WHO AM I?

Self-assessment involves the collection and analysis of data on yourself. Sound simple? It isn't. It is probably easier to assess someone else. In this process, you are putting your life under a microscope to discover who you are, your strengths and weaknesses, your likes and dislikes, your skills and your experiences. In conducting a thorough self-assessment, you will find much about yourself that simple introspection could never achieve. This process should give you a better idea of the types of tasks that you would be good at and be interested in doing. What kind of job responsibilities would make you look forward to getting to work in the morning?

THE EASY WAY OR THE HARD WAY?

There is an understandable tendency for students to take the easy route in the job search: put a résumé together and watch for job postings at the placement office on campus. You must take the time to complete a thorough self-assessment first. When you have completed that step, you will be able to take inventory of your transferable skills. One generic skill might be leadership qualities developed in sports; a more specific skill would be familiarity with the ACCPAC™ accounting software package. You may believe that there is little point in considering the restaurant industry as a career possibility because you have never worked in a restaurant. However, your inventory of transferable skills may include the ability to use cost accounting systems, which may be just what a restaurant chain needs.

When you have inventoried your skills, you will be ready to start your career planning. Given the transferable skills that you determined from your self-assessment, what type of career should you be considering? Is there a particular type of industry that you know really well, or do you have certain skills that would be useful in a broad variety of manufacturing industries? Either way, the process of self-assessment, leading to an inventory of transferable skills, allows you to begin your career planning. To bypass these steps and launch directly into the job-search process is likely to lead to frustration and an inefficient use of your time. Although the self-assessment takes considerable effort, completing it will give you a far better chance of landing not just a job, but the right career job.

FOLLOW THE PROCESS

The first part of the process involves answering the series of questions in Figure 1.1 beginning on page 38. It is critical that you answer these questions honestly because the same answers will be an important guide to your career choice. You might consider having someone who knows you well complete the same assessment of yourself and compare the results.

When the self-assessment worksheets in Figure 1.1 have been completed, the next step is to draw up a ledger of strengths and weaknesses as illustrated in Figure 1.2 on page 45. This is not an easy task and generally requires some reflection. You may seek input from others who know you well. When the first two steps have been completed, prepare a chart of transferable skills (see Figure 1.3 on page 47) and the work or experience that demonstrates your ability to use these skills. Take the time to complete the self-assessment, inventory your skills, and then, using the results, start the career-planning process.

▌▌ Preparing Your Self-Assessment Chart

This first step of self-assessment in the career-planning process is critical. It lays the basic foundation from which you will prepare your résumé and focus your job search. The eight basic areas for self-assessment are:

I Interests
II Aptitudes
III Education
IV Employment Experiences
V Non-Employment Experiences
VI Personality
VII Preferred Job Environment
VIII Personal Goals

The following discussion of these areas will help you think through the questions that appear on the self-assessment worksheet.

INTERESTS

1. *What did I like best about my favourite job?*
- Contact with coworkers?
- Dealing with the public?
- Special assignments?
- Independence that the job provided?
- Knowing exactly what and how each report was to be done?
- Motivating others?

The answers to these and similar questions can give you valuable insight into your own interests. Perhaps you were given the responsibility of studying the trends and preferences of renters at the video rental store where you worked. With little direction from your manager, you studied rentals in the last year and predicted the likely rental activity of new releases. The results of your survey gave the store better guidance on how many copies of a particular release to purchase. Until this opportunity, the work had been dull and routine. You likely found this task satisfying because you worked independently and you discovered that you enjoyed analyzing.

2. *Do I like working with technical things?*

At this point you are not necessarily looking for aptitude or previous experience with technical things but for interest. Although it is obvious the two are related, for now, focus on the level of interest in performing technical tasks. To illustrate this point, one person may have had to spend time repairing their own vehicle because they did not have the financial resources to take the car to the repair shop. A rather common phenomenon for a student! The important point is whether you enjoyed it or not. Some of us enjoy tinkering with lawnmowers or computers, fixing the plumbing, rewiring the house and building cabinets. The importance of this interest, particularly when combined with an aptitude, cannot be overstated. This knowledge of their abilities has aided countless business graduates in selecting and enjoying a very satisfactory career.

3. *Do I enjoy preparing written reports?*

As a business student, you have had to prepare countless reports, essays, assignments, and case studies. Did you enjoy them or dread them? Did the prospect of a formal thirty-page report capture your imagination, or was it just one more assignment needed for the completion of the course? Did you view the project as an opportunity to use your creative talents? Again, different careers have different demands in terms of preparing written reports. However, virtually every job in business requires proficiency in writing.

4. *Do I enjoy working with numbers?*

Again, it is difficult to separate interest from aptitude. You may have strong numeracy skills but find working with numbers to be boring.

Did the project involving the quantitative analysis of a market or the financial analysis of a company's performance rank as your favourite school assignment, or was it something to be endured? Obviously, a student in finance and accounting has an interest (and an aptitude) in numbers, but many other positions in marketing management also include working with numbers. A product manager has to cost out marketing plans in detail and must prepare an economic analysis of a proposed new product. A marketing researcher will find that quantitative analysis is an integral part of the job.

5.   *Do I enjoy using my creative powers?*

Any professor who has worked with students has watched an average and, perhaps, struggling student suddenly catch hold when a project demanding creativity was assigned. Other students simply prefer a more precise, procedurally determined assignment. They need to know the assignment has been completed correctly and they may be frustrated by the more open nature of a project that demands creativity. Accounting demands precision — the work has to do with specifics. Marketing typically requires strong creative skills.

Other questions to ask yourself include: How do you like to spend your leisure time? Do you like travel, reading, sports, being part of a club? The answers to these questions will help to define your interests. It is also important that you list your interests by priority. You might enjoy working with technical equipment but the marketplace might not have openings that require that particular skill. Stay flexible. The market is evolving and will continue to evolve, causing frequent changes in the most sought-after qualifications.

APTITUDES

As already mentioned, aptitudes and interest hold a close relationship. However, being interested in something but having little aptitude for it can be frustrating and may hurt your career. It is important to determine whether or not the aptitude can be developed. It may in fact be easier to develop an aptitude than an interest.

1.   *Do I have good oral communication skills?*

Few positions exist for which oral communication skills are not required. At one time, the stereotype of a typical marketing graduate was that of the "silver-tongued" communicator, someone who had perfected the art of persuasion. The accounting student, on the other hand, was thought to have little need for those same talents. Most business students realize that any position they seek requires strong speaking skills. Admittedly, some positions require presenting or speaking more often than others. When assessing your oral communication skills, it may be useful to categorize your abilities into two areas: one-on-one communication skills, and performance in front of a group. Being good at one does not necessarily mean you will be good at the other. If you are nervous speaking in front of crowds, you have a number of options to overcome this fear. Some people gain confidence from practice; each presentation that goes well reinforces in the speaker the realization that they can speak to groups. If your fear is more intense, you might want to consider public-speaking seminars and courses offered by schools or by such private organizations as Toastmasters. Your school may even have a student chapter of Toastmasters. Being able to add this to your résumé will help to set you apart from the competition.

2.   Do I have good written communication skills?
As a business student, you have most likely taken a communications course. All positions require the basic skills of grammar and punctuation, and a student may be held back from a position if his or her writing ability is poor. As with all of these questions, you must be very honest with your answers. Submitting several samples of your written work to an English or communications teacher for evaluation may help you to gain a realistic appraisal of your written communication skills. Taking extra courses in grammar and writing skills might be helpful if you feel that your writing skills need to be improved.

3.   Do I have an aptitude for technical things?
What does your ability to repair your own car have to do with a career in business? Very little if your career is in the fashion industry. You may, however, work for a company that manufactures production equipment, fork lift trucks, snow blowers, pharmaceutical products, or develops computer software. As a business graduate, you are not being hired to fill the role of an engineer, a technologist or a scientist. However, having an aptitude for technical things means you will have less

difficulty in understanding your employer's technical products and applications. Do you like to "tinker" with your car and did you enjoy any technical courses at high school? Did your family tend to turn to you when something technical or electrical was broken in your house? A student who has difficulty with repairing things or putting together parts that need to be assembled will realize that a job working for a manufacturer of technical products may be too frustrating.

A former student had an old, well-worn vehicle that was the butt of many of his classmates' jokes. He was able to keep it on the road by becoming a regular at the auto wreckers, scrounging for spare parts. He rather enjoyed doing the work. The joking from his classmates stopped when he landed a "plum" job with a major manufacturer of after-market auto parts. The reason this example comes to mind is that he is now a sales manager, and he has just hired another business graduate who likes to tinker with his car!

4.   *How well do I work with numbers?*

Generally speaking, this is one of the easier questions to answer. You have been exposed to mathematics most of your life. Your competency has been evaluated and by now you have a pretty good idea about your abilities. The answer to this question may give you more of a guide on career choice than many of the others. As already stated, basic numeracy skills are needed for almost every job in the business world. The question is whether you have an above-average, average, or below-average aptitude. Accounting, production planning, marketing research, and financial planning are but a few of the occupations that require strong numeracy skills.

5.   *Do I have creative talent?*

Do I perform well when I am assigned a case study in which more is left unsaid than is stated? Am I good at tackling problems for which there are few apparent solutions? Do I consider myself to be an "idea" person? When working in a group, do others tend to turn to me for ideas or would I rather work on the implementation of other people's ideas? Or am I more comfortable when working within guidelines in which procedures and expectations are made clear? Marketing in general, and advertising in particular, need these creative skills.

Do not feel restricted by these questions of aptitude and talent. There are also other areas that reflect what you are best suited for. When considering your character and a possible career, it is useful to consider personal values, spiritual values, and economic restrictions and opportunities.

EDUCATION

Your experience at school and in your personal life provides a valuable insight into who you are. As a business student, you have been exposed to a broad variety of courses that help you focus on a career area.

1.   *What were my best courses? Which ones did I enjoy the most? Why?*

Although most students tend to do best in the courses in which they are most interested, you probably can find some exceptions. Let those courses that you enjoyed the most provide useful information on what holds your interest — that is assuming, of course, that you had reasonably good grades in the courses that you particularly liked. You may have done well on a marketing course but found the content boring. A note of caution — do not confuse a teacher's poor delivery with dull course material.

   Your course of study covers most of the broad areas of business. If a graduate does not find a job interesting and challenging, that job will not develop into a career. It is worthwhile to determine why certain courses were stimulating. The answer to these questions may help you in the first two sections of this personal inventory taking.

2.   *What were my weakest courses? Which ones did I like the least? Why?*

The "why" may be the most important part of this question. Was it a reflection of your lack of interest and/or ability, or was it because of the teacher's delivery method? It is not uncommon for a student to dislike the way a course is taught and then assume that the whole subject is boring. This is a mistake and may result in precluding an area from your job search that might have been rewarding. That aside, if you have consistently not enjoyed and not done well in a series of related courses, you know you must focus on other areas.

3.   *What was my average or grade point average (GPA)?*

It takes only a second to answer that question, but you need to examine the figure more closely. Perhaps your GPA is 2.7 or 63 percent and below class average. Although I am not suggesting that a strong academic average is not a valuable asset, you need to examine other factors. Perhaps you had a part-time job necessitated by financial need. Maybe you played varsity sports or were involved in student government. These and other activities impact on your grades. This is not necessarily a liability. Instead, it may mean that you are a multidimensional person. Most employers have a well-developed talent for looking beyond the numbers. Although some positions do demand a high level of academic performance, other employers allow attitude and hard work to compensate for applicants' lower grades.

4.   *What specific skills have my courses given me?*

You are attending a postsecondary institution because you want to learn new skills, which are an integral part of what you are marketing to potential employers. List these skills and, if possible, be specific. You know how to prepare a financial report and a marketing plan; to program in certain computer languages; to use methods of managing and motivating employees. You have learned a lot, and although you are probably light on practical experience, you have a good understanding of what is required. You may also have completed a few major assignments and had contact with industry while doing these assignments. To help you articulate these skills, refer to your course outlines, which most likely list the course objectives or outcomes.

5.   *What skills have I learned from my extracurricular activities?*

Were you involved in student government or the school newspaper? Did you captain a sports team? Did you participate in a program-related organization such as the American Management Society (AMS)? The richness of college and university life provides many opportunities, and too often students tend to forget their participation as one of their assets.

EMPLOYMENT EXPERIENCE

"All I did was wait on tables." "I stacked the shelves at the local supermarket." As discussed in the introduction to this chapter, you will have acquired skills in your previous job, regardless of how junior or menial they may seem. It is important to closely examine just what you did. For some students, previous work experience may be the best guide to selecting a career area. Students tend to underestimate the skills that previous employment has given them.

1.   *What were my job responsibilities?*

If you waited on tables, you had experience in dealing with the public, often in very trying circumstances. You had to handle cash, and acted as a liaison person between the overworked kitchen and impatient customers. If you stocked shelves at a supermarket, you dealt with customers, and had some responsibility for inventory management. If you had a formal job description, do not use only that to determine your job responsibilities. Most people do many tasks not included in the job description. What happened when new staff were hired? Did you help, however informally, with their training and orientation? During holiday time did you temporarily take on some additional responsibilities? Perhaps you had to close the store and deposit the receipts, work on the accounts payable, order inventory or do countless other tasks that were not a routine part of your job.

2.   *What was I good at? What gave me the most difficulty?*

You may have had experience in dealing with the public but you did not enjoy it and tried to avoid it whenever possible. Obviously, this experience is not an asset except that it can play a critical role in helping you to determine who you are and what you are not. Did you enjoy supervising other people? Were you able to motivate them? Was your work accurate, and completed within acceptable time-frames when you worked in the accounting department? Did you enjoy selling women's clothing in your part-time job and were you good at it? Did you like the unexpected events in your job or did you prefer the set routine? A former student of mine had some supervisory experience with part-time staff in a small discount store. This was not a formal part of her job but it played a major role in a job offer from one of the chartered banks. She had demonstrated an ability to supervise and help organize the work schedule of the part-time high-school students working at the store. The bank viewed this as a critical asset.

3.   *What jobs did I particularly like or dislike?*

Although this question is similar to the previous questions, few jobs are perfect or all bad. To answer this question, look at the total job and determine, on balance, if it was a job you liked and did well or one you were very happy to leave. Why do you feel that way about it? Perhaps you liked the type of work but not the organization. You may have found your duties meaningful but wanted more responsibility for your own actions. Consider your age at the time you had that job. Perhaps at seventeen, you did not like the job. Today, you might.

4. *What transferable skills have I gained from my employment experience?*

You have likely acquired both general skills and specific skills. For example, if you worked in an office you gained insight into office operations and the importance of interpersonal relationships. You may also understand how purchasing, accounting and the secretarial pool interact. If an employer is hiring someone for an entry-level management position, having these aforementioned skills is a definite asset. If you have worked in a factory you have general knowledge of how a production department works, how supervisory and management levels are structured and some material-handling techniques. Other positions may have allowed you to learn about certain products or certain industries. Students who work part time for supermarkets sometimes end up working for a food manufacturer in sales or marketing. While several factors were involved in their successful selection, having a knowledge of food retailing was a transferable general skill.

Many students have also acquired specific skills. You may have a good working knowledge of a particular inventory control system. You may know a particular accounting software package or had sales experience, purchasing experience, supervisory experience. These, and many others, are the transferable skills that could give you an edge over other applicants.

5. *What transferable skills did I learn in my co-op placement?*

If you are one of the growing number of business students enrolled in a co-op program, you have most likely acquired skills that are highly transferable to industry. This type of industry placement should have given you general and specific skills. Employers view co-op students most favourably.

Working in industry on a co-op placement will have exposed you to the general workings of an office. If you were in the accounting department of a meat-packing company, you picked up the relationship between the credit department, the sales department, and production. These are the general skills referred to above. You understand the culture of the workplace, something that can be learned by experience alone. Your work in accounts receivable gave you specific skills in credit management. If you were in the production department, you gained specific skill in production scheduling as well as invaluable knowledge of, and feeling for, production operations.

NON-EMPLOYMENT EXPERIENCE

Every person is shaped by a complex interaction of events in life. Many of the things we do outside school and work also prepare us for our careers. Examining this dimension is a valuable addition to your personal inventory assessment. Some students make the mistake of thinking that if something they do is not school or work experience, it is not relevant.

1. *To what clubs or organizations do I or have I belonged?*

Did your membership in this organization put you in a leadership role? Did you hold office, help with fund-raising? If you are able to answer in the affirmative, you have acquired a transferable skill. If you were a captain of a sports team or participated in Junior Achievement when you were younger, once again you have acquired skills. This type of involvement indicates to an employer that you have well-developed interpersonal abilities. Many corporations show at least as much interest in this dimension of a job applicant's life as they do in school marks.

2. *Do I participate in sports?*

Being an outstanding athlete is not what is particularly important; your participation is what counts. Aside from the obvious benefits of fitness from being involved in sports, your participation has helped make you a multidimensional person. You have learned to deal with competition, to develop teamwork, and how to learn from mistakes. Examine this last statement. Competition, teamwork, learning from mistakes: these terms belong in the business world as much as in the sports world. Understanding and predicting competitive strategies, developing teamwork and learning from mistakes all describe the environment in which business operates.

3. *Have I done any volunteer work?*

Volunteer work may have been done formally or informally. You may have been a designated peer tutor or you may have helped friends with certain courses. You may have helped a charitable organization, a service club, or coached a soccer team. You will have gained experience and increased your versatility by being confronted with new situations. Having done volunteer work says something positive about your character. It may also have given you some specific skills. Two business students I know set up an accounting system for a local charitable organization, stayed to work out the "kinks," and trained the staff in how to use it. This experience gave them a substantial advantage. Although this self-assessment process is designed to inventory what you have already done, consider doing some volunteer work if you have not already done so. It might give you an opening into a career while helping others.

4. *What life experience have I gained?*

All of us have gained life experience, but this question is of particular importance to the mature student. An increasing number of mature students are graduating from postsecondary institutions. It has been my experience that these students often overlook their own assets. You have a head start on younger graduates. You may have balanced raising children, operating the household budget on scarce resources, meeting the demands of school and attempting to have a personal life. Time management, setting priorities and budgeting are a few of the transferable skills acquired. You have also developed a higher level of versatility and flexibility that many younger students do not have. The process of dramatically changing your life-style to return to school and to interact with younger students who have different priorities has solid value. All students have had to develop an ability of setting their own priorities. Several professors gave you projects that were all due at the same time; you were on a sports team and had a part-time job. Without time management and setting priorities, you would not be where you are.

📁 Profile: *Gordon Hsu*

- CURRENT POSITION
  Senior Accountant
  KPMG Peat Marwick Thorne
  Vancouver, British Columbia

- EDUCATION

Chartered Accountant, 1993
Certified General Accountant, 1991
Honours Bachelor of Commerce, 1990, Lakehead University
Bachelor of Business Administration, 1989, Lakehead University
Diploma, Computer Systems, 1983, British Columbia Institute of
Technology

My position at Peat Marwick Thorne is Senior Accountant (fourth year) and my experience as an auditor includes such varied clients as BC Hydro (electrical utility), Concord Pacific Development Inc. (developer of Expo 86 lands) and other significant real-estate-development companies, suppliers to major fast-food chains, and venture-capital corporations. My daily activities may include planning for audits, budgeting, supervising and mentoring staff members, interacting with my firm's partners and client officials, processing personal and corporate tax returns, or forecasting cash flows for a prospectus. My role also includes working as a computer audit specialist, which creates an opportunity to provide a valuable consulting service to my clients.

The accounting and general business courses at Lakehead University gave me the skills to succeed in the accounting field. Lakehead may not be a well-known school, but the accounting program is well respected in the industry. It was a tough program but one that provided a wide range of experiences and knowledge in accounting, audit, finance, computers, operational science and marketing. My studies also included practical off-campus projects, business competition at Queen's University, and barbecues at a professor's home.

Several years before Lakehead University, I had developed another career. Since computers had always interested me, I completed the Computer Systems Diploma in 1983 at British Columbia Institute of Technology (BCIT). BCIT had a significant reputation in the computer field for developing programmers with practical abilities. Several years of part-time programming helped me to thrive in the computer consulting field after my graduation from BCIT. It was the consulting experience that gave me a rare opportunity to start up an EDP department in a new company — Ridley Terminals Inc. (RTI). In 1984, RTI had just completed a $240 million construction of a new coal port in Prince

Rupert and became one of the most efficient and highly mechanized operations in the international coal-port industry. RTI hired me to provide system maintenance, software development and user training on sophisticated and leading-edge computer systems.

With my move to RTI, I began a seven-year trek in the Certified General Accountants' program to broaden my educational background and to provide a general business perspective. Although I still remain intrigued with computers and the "art" of programming, I realized that this was not a life-long career path. (It does not hurt, however, to have both computer and accounting skills on my résumé.) The broader aspects of business was my ultimate goal. I did not have a preferred area of business, but there were skill sets to develop and methods of finding out what piqued my interest. By 1988, I had decided that articling with a large accounting firm would further enhance my business experiences and that obtaining a university degree from Lakehead would help my entry into this profession.

The CA program provided several avenues of opportunities and many of these would be difficult to obtain in industry. Articling at a "Big 6" accounting firm can connect one to future (fellow CA students) and current business leaders. For one week, I could be auditing by myself in a small owner-managed company successfully thriving in a niche market. Other weeks I could be senioring (with a staff of three juniors) a large audit of a Crown corporation. Senior accountants (around third and fourth year at KPMG) provide the on-site leadership to meet the needs of the client and the first line of marketing for the firm's specialized services (i.e., personal and corporate tax, acquisitions and mergers, forensics and personal financial planning).

My future can best be described as being open. I could stay within the firm and remain in audit, specialized in other areas such as acquisitions and mergers, or transfer to another country within the KPMG umbrella and experience a different life-style. If I decide to leave the firm, my experience and skills may lead me to a controllership, financial analyst for a brokerage firm, or owner-manager of a small business.

Athough educational programs are challenging and take serious commitment, the rewards do exist.

◆

PERSONALITY

Although we can change or develop some aspects of our lives, our basic personality is pretty well set. It is important to assess personality carefully, as many careers are clearly more suitable for a certain personality. If you are very shy and do not enjoy meeting new people, a career in sales is obviously not for you. While completing this section, notice that each question is somewhat related to the others.

1. *Am I competitive?*

Do you enjoy the challenge of competition? It may be evident in the sports, marks, and contests. Some competitive spirit is essential to be successful in the world of business, but some areas, such as marketing and sales, demand a stronger sense of competition than others.

2. *Am I particularly sociable?*

This question is not meant to suggest that a person is either sociable or unsociable, but rather, that each of us can be placed on a continuum of sociability. Do you enjoy meeting people? Do you like to be with people or do you prefer to spend more time on individual pursuits? A human-resources manager with weak social skills would represent a real mismatch. A manager of any type without good interpersonal skills will have difficulties. Many students start their first year feeling uncomfortable socially. By joining clubs or organizations, they often overcome this insecurity and gain a lot of confidence and enjoy a social environment.

3. *Do I prefer teamwork or individual work?*

Strongly related to the previous question, the answer here is not an "either/or" but a matter of degree. In fact, for many types of jobs a healthy blend of both is highly desirable. Your preference may be evident in the sports you have played. Do you have a strong preference for such individual sports as running and squash, or do you prefer the teamwork of volleyball, basketball and baseball? Did you like the group projects at school or were the individual projects more to your liking? Most group work involves some friction between participants. How effective were you in resolving the differences within the group? Different careers in business vary in terms of the amount of group work involved; however, an ability to work in teams is a generic skill most employers look for in the business graduate.

4.   *How self-directed am I?*

School experiences and previous employment will help you answer this question. Do I work well with a minimum of supervision or guidelines, or do I prefer to have my task well laid out with established time-lines prepared by my supervisor/professor?

5.   *Am I a leader or a follower?*

Have I taken the initiative on group projects? Do people often expect me to lead the way when planning for a social event? Do I tend to head up committee work? Do I tend to be a class representative? People with leadership skills consistently become captain, chairperson, or spokesperson. They may not seek the role, it just seems to happen. Others prefer to follow, and this should not be viewed as a liability. No organization could operate without capable followers.

6.   *Am I ambitious?*

Certainly any student who has sacrificed a full-time salary, and much more, in order to attend college or university is ambitious. Some of you, however, may have a burning ambition to have a rapid rise in your career. Providing that your expectations are realistic, you will have to seek a career in which this is possible. If you are not in such a hurry and believe the entry-level job will capture your interest for a longer period of time, you should be looking at different career options. It is a common mistake to believe that everyone should be aggressively ambitious. Many people just do not have that as part of their personality. These same people can have a very rewarding career and life-style.

7.   *Do I work quickly at tasks or am I more methodical?*

Some people prefer the opportunity to carefully consider the tasks at hand and to have enough time to steadily work through all the steps, ensuring no mistakes are made along the way. Others thrive in a pressure-cooker environment where there simply is no time to be methodical. They would rather "give it their best shot" quickly and move on to the next task. Again, different careers have different requirements. Being methodical and accurate is a prerequisite for most careers in accounting or data processing. Although it would be naive to suggest there is no time pressure in these areas, accountants and data processors must be methodical and accurate nevertheless.

PREFERRED JOB ENVIRONMENT

1. *What type of supervision do I prefer?*

Do you prefer to be given a lot of "space" by your supervisor? Does the idea of being given a task to be completed in the next month with little or no additional contact with your boss appeal to you? You may, instead, be more comfortable with closer guidance from your employer. The day-to-day contact may give you a feeling of security and reduce the fear of making mistakes.

2. *What hours of work do I want?*

If you are looking for a strict thirty-seven-hour work week, your career choice of business may not have been the best. There are, however, broad differences in the number of hours business graduates work. An important variable is the amount of control you have over the hours you work. Many people in business may work long hours but they can determine just when the hours will be.

3. *Do I want to work for a large company or a small company?*

Are you looking for the prestige and security of a large, nationally known organization? Does the prospect of a formal training program and well-developed fringe benefits appeal to you? Perhaps a small company in which you can make an impact is more to your liking. The smaller company may not have the same defined job description and you may have a highly variable set of duties. In the smaller firm, you may have an opportunity to define, or at least impact on, your own job description. There may also be less security. Referring back to your answers in the personality section may help you in formulating your answers here. Your response to "What hours of work do I want?" may also be a guide. There is a tendency for employees in a small business to work longer hours. Often the small firms cannot wait another day or two to process an order or to finish up a production run.

4. *Would I like to travel as part of my job?*

The amount of travel a business person does is highly variable. Although some occupations such as sales usually require some travel, there are significant differences. Being away from home about 10 percent of the time may appeal to you. If this becomes 40 percent of the time it may become onerous. Perhaps the prospect of travelling a lot in the first few years with the amount diminishing in the future may be what you want. You may start your career in the internal auditing department of a manufacturer with branches spread across the country. Typically you would travel a lot in your earlier years with a significant reduction in travel later on. Many people in business would see this as "paying your dues."

5. Am I willing to relocate?

Are you determined to live in a particular city? For some potential employers this is not a problem. Other organizations will not consider employing someone that cannot or will not relocate. You must consider the nature of the relocation. It may mean the initial position will represent a relocation with little likelihood of subsequent relocation. It is not uncommon for the relocation to happen in the earlier years of a position with permanent residence coming later. Such organizations as banks tend to relocate their employees every few years and, in fact, this movement represents the path to success in the organization.

Often companies with a number of branch locations throughout the country expect geographical mobility from their employees. Companies with defined sales territories may also have the same expectations. Geographical flexibility in tough economic times is a definite asset. Down-turns and restructuring rarely occur equally across the country.

6. What are my salary expectations?

You have worked hard and sacrificed much to become a business graduate. Now you want your rewards. The reaction is understandable even if somewhat unrealistic. Your placement office will be able to give you a general idea on starting salaries. Starting salaries, while important, should be only one of several criteria you use in selecting an organization for potential employment. If the other criteria you have used are positive, do not let the initial salary be an obstacle. Of more significance is the salary you might expect to be making in five years. Even then, other aspects of the job are likely more important. You must also recognize that salaries in the last few years have not had the same growth that was experienced in the eighties. Some industries tend to pay little for entry-level jobs, but offer above-average salaries once employees have proved themselves. The fresh graduate joining a chartered accounting firm or an advertising agency may experience this phenomenon.

7. *What advancement opportunities do I want?*

Do I need to move quickly up the ladder or is a slower, steadier advancement acceptable? Again, it is important to be realistic. Dues have to be paid in every organization. Smaller, aggressive organizations may offer a better chance at rapid advancement. They often offer higher risk as well. When I operated a placement agency I was often asked, "What are the advancement opportunities with your client?" Perhaps the most honest answer in the 1990s is, "It is up to you." Although the speed of advancement may generally vary from industry to industry, most graduates are "captain of their own ship." Advancement often occurs by changing jobs.

PERSONAL GOALS

The most important question to ask yourself is, "What do I want from my career?" Instead of answering several questions as was done in the first few sections, it may be more useful to simply think about what you want out of life and your career. Do you want an all-consuming career in which you can dedicate most of your energies to the job or do you want a position that will provide you with adequate funds to pursue other things you really want out of life? Both positions are somewhat extreme and most likely you fall between the two. You will, however, have to determine in what direction you lean. Consider what you would like to be doing in five or ten years from now, both in your career and in your personal life.

▌▌ Worksheet: Self-Assessment

Now fill in the worksheet in Figure 1.1 on the following pages, making any modifications to the format that might work well for you. In the box at the end of each chart, indicate strategies you could use to overcome potential weaknesses.

For example, in the Interests chart, you may indicate that you do not enjoy preparing written reports. Is that because you have weak written communication skills, or perhaps you are not comfortable with word processing? If so, either is a correctable situation, particularly if you are a first-year student.

Figure 1.1(A). WORKSHEET: INTERESTS

QUESTIONS	ANSWERS
1. What did I like best about my favourite job?	
2. Do I like working with technical things?	
3. Do I enjoy preparing written reports?	
4. Do I enjoy working with numbers?	
5. Do I enjoy using my creative powers?	

STRATEGIES TO BEAT POTENTIAL WEAKNESSES

Figure 1.1(B). WORKSHEET: APTITUDES

QUESTIONS   ANSWERS

1. Do I have good oral
   communication skills?

2. Do I have good written
   communication skills?

3. Do I have an aptitude
   for technical things?

4. How well do I work
   with numbers?

5. Do I have creative talent?

STRATEGIES TO BEAT POTENTIAL WEAKNESSES

Figure 1.1(c). WORKSHEET: EDUCATION

QUESTIONS	ANSWERS

1. Which were my best courses? Which ones did I enjoy the most? Why?

_____

2. Which were my weakest courses? Which ones did I like the least? Why?

_____

3. What was my average or GPA?

_____

4. What specific skills have my courses given me?

_____

5. What skills have I learned from my extracurricular activities?

_____

STRATEGIES TO BEAT POTENTIAL WEAKNESSES

_____

Figure 1.1(D). WORKSHEET: EMPLOYMENT EXPERIENCE

QUESTIONS	ANSWERS
1. What were my job responsibilities?	
2. What was I good at? What gave me the most difficulty?	
3. Which jobs did I particularly like or dislike?	
4. What transferable skills have I gained from my employment experience?	
5. What transferable skills did I learn in my co-op placement?	

STRATEGIES TO BEAT POTENTIAL WEAKNESSES

Figure 1.1(E). WORKSHEET: NON-EMPLOYMENT EXPERIENCE

QUESTIONS	ANSWERS

1. To what clubs or organizations
   do I or have I belonged?

_____

2. Do I participate in sports?

_____

3. Have I done any volunteer
   work?

_____

4. What life experience have
   I gained?

_____

STRATEGIES TO BEAT POTENTIAL WEAKNESSES

Figure 1.1(F). WORKSHEET: PERSONALITY

QUESTIONS	ANSWERS
1. Am I competitive?	
2. Am I particularly sociable?	
3. Do I prefer teamwork or individual work?	
4. How self-directed am I?	
5. Am I a leader or a follower?	
6. Am I ambitious?	
7. Do I work quickly at tasks or am I more methodical?	

STRATEGIES TO BEAT POTENTIAL WEAKNESSES

Figure 1.1(G). WORKSHEET: PREFERRED JOB ENVIRONMENT

QUESTIONS	ANSWERS

1. What type of supervision do I prefer?

2. What hours of work do I want?

3. Do I want to work for a large company or a small company?

4. Would I like to travel as part of my job?

5. Am I willing to relocate?

6. What are my salary expectations?

7. What advancement opportunities do I want?

STRATEGIES TO BEAT POTENTIAL WEAKNESSES

Figure 1.1(H). WORKSHEET: PERSONAL GOALS

QUESTION	ANSWER
1. What do I want from my career?	

▌▌ *Personal Strengths and Weaknesses*

You are now in a position to prepare the second step in the personal inventory-taking process, a ledger of your strengths and weaknesses. Your answers will guide you in preparing this ledger. Input from people who know you well could also prove useful. A "T" chart shown in Figure 1.2 illustrates what the ledger might look like for a particular student.

Figure 1.2. SAMPLE "T" CHART

STRENGTHS	WEAKNESSES
Works quickly	Sometimes impatient
Creative	Not good at detail
Strong oral communication	Slow reader
Aggressive	Poor written communication
Willing to relocate	Gets bored easily
Willing to travel	Dislikes supervision
Willing to work long hours	Limited work experience
Good numeracy skills	Inconsistent grades
Self-confident	
Learns quickly	
Enjoys new and challenging situations	
Participates in sports and activities	
Quick to establish rapport with strangers	

Although it is obvious that you will capitalize on your strengths, you have an opportunity to work on your weaknesses. The sooner you start the process, the greater is the opportunity to take corrective action. Of the eight weaknesses shown in the sample ledger, at least four — slow reader, poor written communication, limited work experience and inconsistent grades — can be improved and even converted into strengths. This will be discussed in more detail later in the chapter.

Remember, preparing the ledger is useful only if you are honest, thorough and objective. Be prepared to spend time assessing your strengths and weaknesses.

▮▮ Transferable Skills

The third step in the personal inventory-taking process is listing your transferable skills and the type of work or experience you have had that demonstrates these skills. One of the major reasons you have selected a business program at a postsecondary institution is that it will offer you a broader selection of career choices. Without that educational background, you are far more likely to be trapped in a job that is not very interesting. Most economists agree that jobs in the nineties are becoming somewhat polarized — low-skill, low-paying service jobs or high-skill, high-paying jobs. Although this may be overstated, the increased polarization is real.

A few years ago, a company that direct-marketed products through catalogue selling would have had a large number of employees working in the warehouse, shipping and receiving. It would also have had a significant accounting staff, inventory control clerks and managers, buyers, supervisors, and printing staff. As well, several researchers would be analyzing the sales of various types of products by geographical region, preparing charts and graphs to help plan new products and delete existing products. Today, that operation may have doubled its sales while retaining only a third of the original staff. The warehouse is computerized with automatic bundling for shipment. The entire mailing list is on a database, which instantly reports which product is selling, where it is selling, and to what kind of client. The inventory system is, of course, interfaced with the database, electronically signalling when additional inventory should be ordered, based upon a given real-time trend analysis. The printing department has been farmed out, or per-haps the company has purchased high-tech composing and printing equipment operated by a sharply reduced staff. This organization uses highly skilled database managers, systems analysts, market researchers, creative writers, and illustrators. The middle layer of inventory mana-gers, accountants, shipping supervisors and others has gone.

As a graduate or soon-to-be graduate of a postsecondary business program, you are likely looking for a career that offers something other than routine and undemanding responsibilities with little opportunity for advancement. Because of your training, you have increased the odds of securing a position that is challenging. But the fact that a job demands a higher skill level and pays well does not mean you will find it stimulating. It must offer the type of responsibility and challenge that is right for you.

Completing the third step on transferable skills will serve several functions. Its primary purpose is, of course, to help direct you to the best career options. It will, however, also be useful when developing a résumé and preparing for a job interview. Remember, transferable skills are those skills that you have acquired that will be useful in certain types of careers. There is little point in doing any career planning until you have completed your inventory of transferable skills. Figure 1.3 is an abbreviated example of the transferable skills chart. Using this chart will be your guide to listing your transferable skills. Please note the relationship between "skill" and "how demonstrated." You may have had some particular achievement associated with a skill. Detail these achievements in the third column, as this information will also be useful for your résumé and job interviews. When you reach the chapter on résumé writing, this relationship will be critical.

Figure 1.3. TRANSFERABLE SKILLS

SKILL	HOW DEMONSTRATED	ACHIEVEMENT
Numeracy skills	Good grades in maths, statistics, and quantitative methods courses	

Analytical skills	Did well in case study, financial analysis	Our group won top second-year case-analysis award, "Establishing a Physical Distribution System for a Small Manufacturer"
Works well with others	Summer jobs involved team approach to completing work assignments	Only time a complete team was recommended for rehiring for next summer
Leadership skills	Did well when made temporary supervisor on last job; captain of soccer team	Won district soccer championship
Oral communication	Successful teaching of swimming lessons	
Mechanical aptitude	Enjoy repairing my own car	
Well-organized	Balanced responsibilities of being a parent, part-time job, and school	Able to maintain top-third-of-class status
Artistic/graphic art skills	Volunteer work required art skills, preparing posters, designing logos	
Persuasive skills	Strong sales figures working for commission at Home Electronics Store	Top part-time sales person during Christmas season
Working knowledge of French and Spanish	Was in French Immersion for 11 years and have taken 3 conversational Spanish courses	

EXAMINE YOUR LIABILITIES

Now that this fairly lengthy process is almost complete, it may be useful to go through the somewhat painful experience of examining your liabilities. You should be able to put these liabilities into one of two categories; those that can be improved and those that cannot. If you are weak in oral communication you can definitely improve those skills, often dramatically. If you have always worked slowly, but carefully, this will not be easy to change. Other liabilities simply are not liabilities in certain careers. Recognizing that fact has been the point of going through the three-step process outlined in this chapter. Here are some examples of liabilities that are not necessarily liabilities.

- *"I have little job experience."*

While having job-related experience is unquestionably an asset, most employers do not expect you to have directly related experience. You have learned much in school that will help you on the job and you know that your learning has just started in this entry-level position. When employers are hiring recent graduates, they are hiring potential. Many companies believe it is easier to mould those employees who do not have preconceived ideas.

- *"The position I am looking for does not relate very closely to the courses I have taken."*

You have received a broadly based education. Most postsecondary programs in business are designed to give you a blend of general knowledge and specific skills. Part of any program is to develop thinking and analytical skills in the graduate. That, coupled with good communication skills, may be the most important selection criteria to the recruiters.

- *"My grades are not in the top 25 percent."*

Why not? Perhaps you had a demanding part-time job that eroded the time available for school work. You had this job because you were financing in part, or in total, your educational costs. Virtually every potential employer can understand this and, in fact, most would view you as having a real asset. You have had to work hard to get to where you are now. Maybe you played a varsity sport, were a member of the student council, or participated in other extracurricular activities. Most professors have heard employers stress the advantages of hiring the well-rounded person. These students usually have better developed interpersonal skills and have gained experiences that give them transferable skills.

▮▮ Conclusion

You now should have a far better idea of who you are and what you have to offer. You should understand that you are not an average student. No such person exists. You have strengths that you will use to your advantage. You will either improve your weaknesses or focus your career search in those areas where your weaknesses are not liabilities.

Although business graduates enter an extremely broad variety of positions, each requiring somewhat different skills, there are certain generic skills that almost all employers are looking for. If you are weak in analytical thinking, have difficulty with either oral or written communication, are not comfortable with word processing, electronic spreadsheets, and at least some of the more basic graphic software packages, you are at a distinct disadvantage. The good news is that all these problems are correctable. As discussed earlier in the chapter, there are courses available in your curriculum, through continuing education, or through a multitude of private organizations that will allow you to develop and strengthen these requisite skills. As most readers are aware, taking these extra courses will be part of your life-long learning. Any successful career in business will be accompanied by continuous learning, including both formal and informal training.

This chapter opened with an employment "Wanted" advertisement asking for "a bright, energetic person who has demonstrated leadership skills and works well with people. Strong communication skills, a well-developed sense of organization, and self-direction are essential qualities for anyone applying for this position." Perhaps now that you have completed the personal inventory-taking process, you realize that this advertisement is indeed directed to you.

🗁 Profile: *Viki Young*

- CURRENT POSITION

  Consultant
  Monitor Company
  Toronto, Ontario

- EDUCATION

  Bachelor of Commerce (First Class Honours),
  1991, Queen's University

I am a consultant at a young, dynamic firm in Toronto, the Monitor Company. Monitor specializes in strategy consulting, which is one aspect of management consulting. As a consultant, I work in a relatively unstructured and collegial environment on teams that typically range in size from four to eight members. The types of projects I work on vary tremendously. For example, specific cases include: developing category strategy for a major Canadian retailer; creating an overall positioning strategy for an automotive-parts manufacturer; designing new product-development and market-entry strategy for a telecommunications company.

As these examples illustrate, diversity is inherent in the role of a consultant. Clients span different industries; the nature of the client problem requires unique approaches; team members change from project to project. Over the course of two years, my role has evolved from executing on specific analyses to actually designing the analysis itself and leading sections or modules within a larger project.

Although it is difficult to portray an "average" day, there are a number of activities that are common to each project. As one component of the overall project, I identify the analytical steps required to make a specific business decision. I then work, perhaps, with more junior consultants to make sure the correct data is gathered and the analysis is completed. The final stage is the integration of the work contributed by each team member to form a comprehensive answer for the client.

I initially joined the company between my third and fourth years of university as a summer student in the first summer program at Monitor, and later received an offer for a permanent position. Summer internships provide valuable insight into the realities of a potential job and provide an opportunity for students and prospective employers to assess how well they fit together.

I discovered that strategy consulting was a natural fit with the program I chose to follow at Queen's. Although the Commerce program encourages students to specialize in particular functional areas, (i.e., marketing, finance, accounting, industrial relations / human resources, and production), I was more intrigued by the integration of these functional areas — business policy or strategy. My job now provides the opportunity to utilize existing knowledge and to gain new skills in each of these fields.

One of the primary benefits I derived from the Commerce program at Queen's was the teamwork incorporated into each course. In an academic setting, teamwork is relatively unique in a business faculty; however, it is both crucial and prevalent in the business environment.

Another valuable opportunity offered at Queen's was the extracurricular activities. As chairperson of a number of different committees and vice-president of the Commerce Society, I became involved with campus issues, promoting student interests, contributing to the faculty of business and student life, and not least of all, making some very good friends. In addition, extracurricular involvement proved to be an asset when job recruiting began in fourth year. Recruiters tend to look for students who have demonstrated leadership and initiative, who can handle a demanding work load, manage time effectively, and can successfully juggle different tasks at once.

I have tried to maintain this same variety of interests since graduation and have become involved in volunteer tutoring for single mothers who have returned to high school to complete their diplomas.

My future plans consist of pursuing an interdisciplinary Master's degree in public policy and the field of higher education after my tenure at Monitor Company. Ultimately, I would like to attain a Ph.D. related to postsecondary education policy. My vision lies in being involved in the evolution of the Canadian postsecondary education system as a key component to the structural change in the Canadian economy.

◆

RESEARCHING THE JOB MARKET

📁 **Profile:** *Keith M. Colbourn*

- CURRENT POSITION

  Account Manager
  Sponsor Development & Marketing Group
  Loyalty Management Group Canada Inc.
  Toronto, Ontario

- EDUCATION

  Bachelor of Commerce (Honours), 1991,
  Queen's University

LMGC started in June 1991 with three employees. Their mission was to launch the first-ever, cross-category customer loyalty program in

Canada. The concept was simple: offer consumers a desirable incentive to purchase from certain companies; make joining free; make participation hassle free; and by signing up a variety of noncompeting businesses, make it easy for the consumer to attain the award and cost effective for the participating companies. The AIR MILES™ Reward Program was launched on March 30, 1992, with twelve Charter Sponsors, including many of the biggest names in the Canadian marketplace (Bank of Montreal, Sears, Safeway, etc.). Since then, it has grown and grown and grown. Now, on the second birthday of AIR MILES, over 3.5 million Canadian households are collecting travel miles and eighty-five sponsoring companies are issuing miles to their customers.

I joined LMGC in February 1992 as its first Business Analyst. At first, tasks varied wildly with marketing, finance, sales, operations, human resources (interviewing someone who has been in business longer than I had been alive provided great learning), and corporate strategy projects all ending up on my desk.

With all these tasks came the "other" side of a start-up operation: no corporate infrastructure. If something needed doing, there was no HR department to go to, no purchasing group (I once found myself on the street buying VCRS for the Board of Directors meeting the next day) and no one to turn to and ask, "When this was done last year, what did it look like?" or "What mistakes were made?" Everything was new, and as much as it was exciting, it could also get frustrating.

Working within a growing company allowed me to grow quickly as well. I was promoted to Account Executive in April 1993 and then Account Manager in October 1993. For the past year, most of my duties have centred around sales and account management.

Working at LMGC has been similar to my education. The Queen's University Commerce program does not require specialization in a particular major and thus allows the student to gain a broad view of business. A further strength was its combination of theory and practice, in part through case studies and consulting for the business community.

Maybe one of the greatest contributions the school gave me, and probably the most underestimated, was basic business skills, particularly computing, which allowed me to contribute immediately to the company. Extracurricular activities also enabled me to contribute more quickly than I might have otherwise, especially in the area of problem solving.

After graduating, I had pursued a number of small, entrepreneurial ventures. Starting and running such ventures has, for as long as I can remember, been one of my dreams. Initially, it was a difficult decision to pursue my entrepreneurial desires instead of working for a large company. In many ways there are unwritten subtexts encouraging graduates, particularly business graduates, to join the big corporate world. The many other available experiences and opportunities sometimes don't get that same exposure as the high-profile corporate jobs.

The people at LMGC are incredible and we work very much as a team. This has provided me with insight: in the same way a professor can make a course, people can make a company. As I reflect on the last two years, it is this fact that strikes me as the most important. Yes, the business is a great success and there have been many accomplishments. I am, however, most thankful for having the opportunity to work with such wonderful people. Life is made up of moments and memories, and LMGC has given me many.

◆

I I *Introduction*

"When I graduate, I think I'll work for Procter & Gamble as a product manager." "I'm going to work for the human resources department at Xerox." "I'm going to be a financial analyst at Bell Canada." Twenty years ago, a student could make such statements and not be laughed at. Today, such statements tend to show a naiveté and an inflexibility that does not match the realities of the business world of the nineties.

Although the global restructuring of economies has reduced the number of jobs, other factors have had an even more profound impact. Change is one of the few constants in industry. Just as many of the products sitting on a supermarket shelf did not exist five years ago, many of the job responsibilities you may hold in five years might not exist at present. Any business student's career planning must involve flexibility. For decades, students have heard repeatedly that they must have goals and that they should focus on their goals. Although goals obviously still play an integral part in career planning, they must not become a straitjacket that prevents you from thinking about opportunities previously not considered.

Just as your self-assessment described in the previous chapter will have indicated additional courses you should take to make yourself more competitive, so will the career-planning process. Again, the concept of life-long learning must be stressed. Not only will your newly acquired knowledge strengthen your chances, you may also find that it broadens your perspective on career planning. One of my former students recognized the obvious trend to export marketing. A government agency sponsored a one-day seminar on export opportunities. She attended (at a discount student price) and found the day very exciting. With her appetite whetted, she took an additional evening course on export marketing. Today, she is the export manager for a manufacturer of wheelchairs and other assistive devices. Neither the employer nor the type of work she is now doing would have shown up on her list of preferred companies and jobs prior to attending that seminar.

Even in a strong economy, career planning is important. In today's business climate, it is essential. Every graduating student has strengths and transferable skills and must plan for a career in which these strengths and skills can be utilized. In marketing terms, each person has a differential advantage — something that sets them apart from the pack. It could be a "soft" skill such as leadership qualities, or a "hard" skill such as expertise in dBase IV, or considerable experience in selling sporting equipment. With strong competition for career jobs, the match of your skills to the requirements of a particular job is important. Without that match, you may be one of dozens competing for the position with little to distinguish you from the others.

By following the steps outlined in this book so far, you have prepared your own personal inventory. You have identified your strengths and weaknesses and have listed your transferable skills. Those steps should now play a significant role in your career-planning strategy. The dictum "know thyself" has been obeyed. The ideal job for you will make the most of your experiences, interests, and personal skills. Sounds easy. It isn't. It was not easy preparing the personal inventory, but it was worth it. That step in the process required introspection, or internal research. The next step requires external research — an examination of the job market. You will have two objectives during this phase: (1) to determine general business trends that will uncover opportunities that are emerging in the nineties; and (2) to determine which types of skills are needed for certain types of career positions.

▐▌ Business Trends and Opportunities

This section identifies some general trends that are emerging in Canadian business. They are not presented as a comprehensive listing of all trends. Your geographical area may be offering different opportunities. Routine reading of both the regional and local business press as well as the national press will help you to identify emerging opportunities. If you live in a region of Canada where the economy is resource-based, study what is happening in those industries. A note of caution! While you may determine that a certain industry is rebounding or emerging, this does not necessarily translate into career opportunities. It is obvious, however, that career potential is greater in growing industries than in declining ones.

Studies have shown that manufacturing employment has gone through major changes in the last thirty years.[1] Wealthy nations, such as Canada, have a smaller proportion of their total employment in manufacturing, while the emerging nations of Asia have a larger proportion in manufacturing. That does not mean we are manufacturing less, but, rather, we are moving to higher productivity through automation, while labour-intensive manufacturing gravitates toward areas of lower labour rates. The North American Free Trade Agreement provides even more impetus to this trend, and this situation has a significant impact on opportunities for business graduates.

Reading some of the many business publications focused on current and projected business development is one method of researching business trends. Several publications such as *Canadian Business*, *Financial Post*, *The Globe and Mail*'s "Report on Business" and *Marketing* do a good job of reporting on business trends at the national level. There are several regional publications that focus more on local trends. Read these publications; your library has them. If you can afford to subscribe to them, do it. They will be an invaluable aid in career planning as well as offering all kinds of benefits to you as a business student. Most of these publications offer special student rates of up to 50 percent off the regular subscription price.

When you pick up a business magazine, the daily newspaper, or watch the evening news, certain words reappear with increasing frequency; "downsizing" and "restructuring" are examples of words you can hear daily. Any business student understands what these words mean — fewer jobs. A more detailed examination of the same articles or reports will, however, show that the problem is not necessarily shared equally by all types of industry. Although it would be a disservice to the reader to paint a rosy picture of employment possibilities, there are many opportunities. As a business student, you are most likely aware that some sectors of the economy, certain industries and particular types of positions do offer a stronger future than others.

Nuala Beck, president of Nuala Beck & Associates and author of *Shifting Gears: Thriving in the New Economy* (Toronto: HarperCollins Canada Ltd., 1992), recently told a group of economic development officials that Canada has two economies, the old economy and the new economy, but that most Canadians do not understand the difference. She said the new economy, which represents future growth, includes "computers and semi-conductors, health and medical services, communications and telecommunications, and the design and production of instrumentation."[2] It is the new economy that will drive the economy into the next millennium.

▮▮ Identifying the Growth Industries

THE AGING POPULATION

Health-care costs have resulted in governments cutting back on funding. Budget cuts at hospitals, with layoffs of their professional staff, are endemic. It would seem to be an area that any graduate should avoid. Nothing could be further from the truth. Health care is a growth industry and will continue to be for decades to come. It does offer career opportunities for business graduates. The fact that there are severe budget restrictions will create these opportunities. Preventative medicine will stimulate the growth of such new industries as exercise equipment and health-oriented foods. These growth industries will need managers, salespeople, and accountants. Pharmaceutical companies will prosper as our population ages. So will the nursing-home industry.

Our aging population will also stimulate other growth industries, including travel, recreation, and accommodation. None of these growth industries can successfully compete without the skills that the business graduate can bring to their organization.

This "greying" of Canada has spawned another growth in retirement and financial-planning services. In Canada, the universality of social programs is clearly under attack. Few middle-aged people believe they can rely on government pensions and they are seeking alternatives to plan for their retirement years. Trust companies, life insurance companies, investment-planning companies, and tax advisors have been experiencing, and will continue to experience, strong growth.

THE INFORMATION HIGHWAY

Communications is another obvious growth industry. The need for equipment and services is evolving rapidly and is creating new and exciting career opportunities, not just for engineers and technologists, but also for accounting, management, and marketing graduates. Facsimile, cellular phones, and voice mail are but a few of the products and services enjoying growth.

ENVIRONMENTAL MARKETS

The strong growth of environmental products is viewed as being in its infancy. The products considered to be environmentally sound and the multitude of products designed to control pollution will enjoy strong growth throughout the nineties and well into the next century. Businesses dealing with environmental products are considered to be one of the most important job creators, providing some of the most attractive career opportunities in the job market.

THE GROWING SMALL BUSINESSES

Perhaps less obvious are those companies that have found a niche either by developing a unique technology or by finding a previously unfulfilled need in the marketplace. They can often be found in almost any industrial category. With the signing of the Canada-United States Free Trade Agreement and NAFTA, most economists believe these "niche" industries will be the success stories of this and succeeding decades. It is an important part of your career planning to identify those organizations that are poised for this kind of success.

One of our local companies has a total work force of about fifty. They manufacture high-tech packaging equipment and export their products to Europe and the United States. In the last four years, they have hired five business graduates, and they are a high-tech company of just fifty employees!

To illustrate the growing importance of small business in job creation, consider the following statistics. In 1979, 40.8 percent of all working Canadians were with firms that had fewer than 100 employees. By 1989, this number had reached 47.1 percent. When considering net changes in employment, that is, new positions created versus those eliminated, virtually 100 percent of the net gain came from small business (fewer than 100 employees.)[3]

Some graduating students tend to focus on the larger, well-known organizations. These companies have had a poor record of job creation. In your job search, it is wise to give serious consideration to small entrepreneurial organizations, along with thorough research into small businesses. Small businesses have hired more people recently than have large businesses. Some may also become large companies. Participating in those growth years can be exciting and rewarding.

BEYOND OUR OWN BORDERS

A recent article in the *Financial Post*, "Wall Street Takes Shine to Canadian Graduates,"[4] outlines how United States financial-sector companies are dramatically increasing their recruitment on Canadian campuses, with investment bankers, financial consulting firms, and assurance companies at the forefront. The University of Western Ontario and the University of Calgary reported a high level of recruiting activities by United States firms. Canada is strong in the area of undergraduate business programs, while the United States, by comparison, does not have many. Often firms in the United States hire personnel for entry-level positions, so there is a natural link-up with Canadian business graduates. Graduates in the United States more typically have a liberal arts degree.

STARTING YOUR OWN BUSINESS

Many business students have seriously considered starting up their own business. This is another option to consider, but it is certainly beyond the scope of this book to explore the intricacy and challenge of entrepreneurship. Most successful entrepreneurs do not start a business without a solid background of experience, something most graduating students do not yet have. Many companies contract out work, however, and you may have the requisite skills to do contract work. Perhaps you are particularly skilled at setting up an accounting software package or you are competent in inventory systems and control. These, or a combination of other strengths you may have, could be useful on a contract basis to many firms.

Three of my marketing students completed a major primary research project as part of a course requirement. This involved developing a research proposal for a client company and seeing the project through to the final presentation of the report to a group of the senior executives. The executives were very impressed and surprised by the quality of the students' work. Originally, they had agreed to let the students complete the project in order to be good corporate citizens. They did not realize that students were capable of doing such a professional job — they had paid thousands of dollars to have a similar study done by a marketing-research organization. That comment stimulated the students' thinking. "If we are that capable, surely there are other companies that might be able to use our talents." They knew that most organizations did little, if any, primary research themselves — they contracted out this work to marketing-research organizations.

The students' next line of logic came from what all business students learned in their first year: "Who supplies this service?" "How could we compete against them?" "What differential service could we offer?" The answers were almost as straightforward as the questions. Large, nationally well-known market-research companies do much of the business. Any company needing a national study would automatically turn to them. However, a client company might want to know more about the attitude of shoppers going to a mall in Burnaby, British Columbia. Or perhaps a regional mall wants to know what percentage of their customers use the mall as their primary shopping centre, as opposed to occasional use. These examples represent fairly small studies. Who better to do them than a small, local marketing-research company that knows the local area, one that can react quickly and operates with very little overhead? To conclude this story, the three students set up a research company, and had as their first client the same organization they worked with on their school project. Since then, they have added several more clients, moved to a bigger office and added more staff—all in less than a year.

It would be very misleading to suggest these three students' enterprise went as easily as I have described. Every new business experiences growing pains and this one is no exception. However, by using a niche-marketing philosophy they found an opportunity and created their own jobs. For business students with a strong background in accounting or in computers, similar niche-marketing opportunities exist. My wife was an executor for the estate of a deceased relative, which involved a lot of complex accounting for tax purposes. She used a business graduate from our accounting program who had taken an extra course in estate taxation. He accepted my wife's business as a favour to me; now he is at the saturation level.

CONTRACT HIRING

There is a marked tendency toward hiring people on a contract basis. This is not the same as contracting out work, which means you work independently, frequently out of your own home. In a short-term contract, you are hired for a certain period of time to fulfill a certain task. There may be some tendency on your part to shy away from that type of offer. Reconsider! You will have an opportunity to gain valuable experience and sharpen those skills that got you the offer in the first place. It is likely to make your next job-search easier. If you do get the chance of a contract position, you may be able to convert it into a full-time job.

Sometimes a company will hire on a contract basis without any intention of making the position permanent. This same company may be very reluctant to let the contract expire and lose someone who has turned out to be a valuable employee. In other cases, the company may have the option of offering a contract employee a full-time position. In any case, the contract position could have full-time possibilities. You may also find, after having held contracts with several different companies, that you really prefer this to full-time permanent employment. You may be gaining better and broader experience than you would in working for one employer. This type of employment may also lead you down the path to entrepreneurship. At some point you may ask yourself, "Why don't I do this as an independent consultant?" This transition blends well with the business trend of the nineties — companies like to stay "lean and mean" and keep the number of permanent staff low.

THE MANAGEMENT-TRAINING PROGRAM

One outcome of companies downsizing to become lean and mean is the de-emphasis of the management-training program. Commonly in the seventies and eighties, large companies hired graduates and placed them in their management-training program. This often lasted a few years and might involve moving the newly hired graduate from department to department, interspersed with formal training sessions.

The theory behind this was that the company could help the new recruit develop over time and eventually the employee would become a contributing member of the organization. The lean-and-mean philosophy has demanded a closer look at the bottom line, and recruiters are looking at applicants more in terms of what they can do for the company now.

📁 Profile: *Andrew Lue Pann*

- CURRENT POSITION
  Marketing Coordinator
  Excelle Brands Food Corporation
  Weston, Ontario
- EDUCATION
  Business Management, Marketing,
  Bachelor of Business Management, 1992,
  Ryerson Polytechnic University

I work for Excelle Brands Food Corporation as a marketing coordinator in the Food Service Division. Excelle Brands is a small to mid-size manufacturer of salad dressings and sauces. I work closely with the director of marketing and the president to formulate strategies to achieve our company objectives and goals. Our sales force in the food-service division is comprised of several brokers across Canada, who channel our products through distributors to the end users. One of my responsibilities is to aid the director of marketing in managing our brokers' activity by performing sales analysis and comparing their actual sales with their forecasted projections. As well, I am responsible for supporting our brokers by attending national and local trade shows, supplying sales material and samples, and delivering presentations to potentially large customers.

I owe my job to Ryerson Business School, as I was able to show my skills to the president of this company through the development of a marketing plan for his firm as a mandatory class assignment. For example, studying production models and systems at university gave me the tools to analyze Excelle's production and manufacturing process. My courses there gave me an in-depth understanding of business. The Ryerson Business School combines theory and practice for every application of business. Students graduate with a strong understanding of computers, finance, production, management, and marketing. Ryerson's case-method approach was very intensive and challenging as we were constantly given a hands-on opportunity to apply our theoretical knowledge, test our strategical thinking, and sharpen our communication skills.

After graduation, I moved to Cincinnati, Ohio, for five months to work for the Canadian Government Trade Office. This opportunity was granted to me through my involvement with an association on campus called AIESEC. AIESEC, a French acronym for International Association of Students in Economics and Commerce, is a global organization that links students around the world who have a common goal — internationalism. As vice-president of AIESEC at Ryerson, I managed 40 students in promoting internationalism to Toronto's business community as well as on campus.

At the Canadian Government Trade Office as trade assistant, I assisted the Federal Trade Consul in consulting to Canadian firms that wished to export to the United States. I conducted many industry analyses, became more familiar with the Canada-United States Free

Trade Agreement (FTA) and the North American Free Trade Agreement (NAFTA), organized Canadian pavilions at American trade shows, and set up initial meetings with Canadian and American firms for possible strategic alliances.

In my experience, I have found that people who have mastered the skills of communicating clearly and concisely are the people who tend to receive a lot of respect. Whether it is with your clients, managers, peers or subordinates, strong written and verbal communication skills are mandatory to be successful. For this reason I would highly recommend communication courses to any person in any position.

My marketing and overall business background opened the gate to many avenues and potential directions in which I can travel. My short-term goal is to play an integral part in the launch of our new product-line of portion pouches. My personal long-term goal is to establish my own company with products or services that are demanded internationally.

◆

■ What Skills Are Businesses Looking For?

The second objective in your career planning strategy is to determine the types of skills that are needed for certain types of career positions. This is a bit tougher and will require more work on your part. The single best way to do this is to talk to people in those growing industries that you identified in the previous phase. For many of you, this may be the first time you have had to contact someone in business and ask for a favour. You do have a tremendous asset, however. You are a student! Most people in industry will be helpful when a student contacts them in order to find out what skills/qualities are required for certain types of positions in their company. You may know somebody, or know somebody who knows somebody, in that company. Use your contacts. Perhaps your professor knows somebody in the organization. Is there a graduate from your school working there? If your existing network cannot uncover a contact, then "cold-call" the company and get the name of the person for whom you would be likely to work or who would hire you. Once you have the name, make the contact and explain that you are a student at .... and would like an opportunity to discuss what companies are looking for in a graduate. If you receive a "Well, we're not looking for anyone right now," just restate that you are not looking for a job; you just want to research the job for your career planning. It is hard to turn down that request.

JOB SHADOWING

A variation of this approach is to enquire about the possibility of job-shadowing an employee who is doing the type of work that you are interested in. This really can give you valuable insight into the job, and help you determine how this job matches up with the strengths and transferable skills you identified earlier. If the job-shadowing extends beyond one day, it is even more valuable.

Some of our students, as part of a course requirement, do have to shadow someone. They are also expected to set this up on their own. After completing the shadowing assignment, one of my students was driving through an industrial basin and spotted a manufacturer that he had heard of, but knew little about. On impulse, he stopped in and asked to speak to the sales manager to arrange another job shadowing. The sales manager's first comment was, "Where's your résumé?" Although taken aback, the student quickly recovered and dug out a résumé. Three interviews later he received and accepted a job offer.

MOCK INTERVIEW

Mock interviews, which are discussed on page 82, can also give you an idea of what skills a company is looking for. The discussion between you and the interviewer after the interview usually involves a review of the company's needs when hiring a graduate in your selected area. These mock interviews are primarily designed to give students an opportunity to sharpen their interview skills. At the same time, they are an effective way to research the skills required in different career jobs.

Avoid any tendencies toward being unprofessional. As a professor, I have had somewhat embarrassing conversations with employers who have given students an opportunity, and who then told me that the student was not wearing business attire or was late for the appointment. The next point is critical. *Treat the opportunity for an informational or mock interview as though it were real.* You never know — it might be.

Last year, four students arranged mock interviews at a chartered bank. One of the interviewers graduated from our school nine years ago, and the other was a member of a Program Advisory Committee, a group of people from industry who help us in curriculum design. Because of the interviewers' background, all four of the students should have realized that there would be a favourable climate with some potential for a career with the bank. Two of the students treated the process as an exercise, the other two as a real job interview. The latter two researched the bank, had their résumés well prepared, dressed for the part and were able to ask well-informed questions. They sent thank-you letters immediately after the interview, indicating their strong interest. They were both eventually hired. The others learned a lesson, based on the feedback that the interviewers gave us.

These contacts may be the start of your networking, your building of contacts. Make a good impression, keep in touch, and you may have created a job opportunity.

INFORMATIONAL INTERVIEWS

Informational interviews involve the student interviewing potential employers to determine the skills they look for in a business graduate. It is often easier to set up the informational interview, the job shadow, or the mock interview if your school placement office helps with the arrangements. Or perhaps a professor could integrate the interview with one of your courses and help to make the arrangements. If this advantage does not exist at your school, set up the appointments on your own. Research as many different types of job as time allows. These same techniques are discussed in this book under "Making Contacts" on page 77.

GENERIC SKILLS

Although each industry has its particular skill demands and you must try to match these with your particular skills and strengths, certain requirements are becoming somewhat generic. Industry has often expressed these requirements by relating what they see lacking in today's graduates. Research the business press in your own library. You will find many articles quoting disgruntled business people when asked about today's business graduates. A gold-medal winner in accounting will not help a company if they have weak interpersonal skills. That graduate will be working with other people and will invariably be part of a team. The notion that it is only the sales/marketing people who need to have strong oral communication skills is as antiquated as a desktop calculator. *All* graduates must have strong written-communication skills. An ineffectively written report to your manager is the kiss of death. I am sure most readers recognize that computer literacy is essential, but less obvious is the need for logical thinking skills. Employers know that with change as the only constant, strong, critical thinking skills are necessary for any business person. The other essential generic skill is flexibility. As stated before, constant change demands flexibility in employees. The idea of learning your job and then "settling in" to a comfortable routine has no place in the business world.

Obviously, industry wants those people who can contribute quickly and who will be able to adapt to inevitable change. Although much of the material you are covering in your business courses may become outdated in the next few years, it does provide you with a background in understanding the upcoming changes, and will prepare you for life-long learning.

MISSING SOME OF THE SKILLS?

When you match up your skills with the skills required in different positions, it is not uncommon to find that you have, say, 80 percent of the requisite skills. Obviously, no postsecondary business program can teach all skills for all jobs. Your experience has added others, but some may be still missing. A continuing education course may be the solution. Was there a particular software package needed? Were they looking for strong presentational skills? Did they want a basic understanding of chemistry? Is your high-school French pretty rusty? Continuing education courses at your school or at the high school, or membership in an organization such as Toastmasters, may increase the match of your skills with the requirements of a career in which you are interested. Taking these additional courses or training can be the start of a lifetime of learning, enabling you to adapt to the profound changes that are continuous in the business world you will be entering.

■■ Conclusions

It would be a worthwhile exercise to contact ten people in career areas in which you are interested and interview them. Ask them what led to their current position and if they envisioned doing this kind of work just five years ago. You might also ask them what particular skills enable them to successfully perform the type of work they do. Their answers may serve as a valuable guide in helping you plan your career choice. Do not be at all surprised if some of them tell you they had no idea they would be doing this kind of work.

Although this guide on career planning is directed toward the launch of your business career, it could also prove useful when you reevaluate your career later on — again, something that is almost inevitable.

🗁 Profile: *Michelle Lewis*

- CURRENT POSITION

  Research Analyst
  Adults Only Video
  Kitchener, Ontario

- EDUCATION

  Business Administration, Marketing, 1994,
  Conestoga College

I work for a Kitchener firm that uses one of the fastest growing marketing applications to help it reach its customer base. Specifically, I operate a software program called ConquestCanada, which is a compilation of databases combined with mapping capabilities. The software is owned by Compusearch Marketing Data and Systems, one of the pioneers in database marketing in Canada. They lead the industry because of the precision and depth of the information they can provide.

Through manipulation of the data, I can evaluate existing or potential retail site locations, rank markets, determine market penetration, and profile customers' life-styles or buying habits, including the magazines to which they subscribe and what television shows they watch.

I work directly for the client who has leased Conquest and not for Compusearch. The minimum time the program can be leased is 12 months; however, my contract is currently for only six months.

The client for whom I work is Adults Only Video. AOV is one of the fastest growing retailers in Canada. Because it is a video chain and memberships are required, AOV has extensive customer information. I can import this customer or sales data or competitor information to provide AOV with a more accurate picture of the marketplace.

What I do on a daily basis is quite varied. I work with a number of people such as the sales manager, the real estate manager, and the president to find out what information they need to help them make their decisions. The most challenging part of my job is the conceptual aspect of Conquest. The applications are limitless, which makes the task of finding the relevant use of the data difficult. I have to be as accurate as possible, while also being concise because the people to whom I present the information want the "bottom line."

In retrospect, I can see how the education at Conestoga College has helped in shaping my career plan. The courses gave me a solid marketing background for such different applications as retailing and advertising. The hands-on experiences and the research work that we had to do in our third year provided me with the reality of the business world and a working knowledge that proved invaluable.

A faculty member at Conestoga College knew of my interest in marketing research and mentioned Compusearch and I decided to apply. After countless bouts with voice mail, I finally contacted a real person. I told them who I was, what my education was, that I had read up on and researched their company, that I loved what they did and wanted to be a part of it. I believe I was given an interview because of the enthusiasm I had for the industry and company, and because I took the initiative and was persistent. Having a strong relationship with the marketing faculty at Conestoga is probably the main reason I am where I am today. I knew I had to do research in my job hunt, but the faculty members gave me direction as to who to contact as well as motivating me to make the initial contact.

My short-term future plan is to continue to pick up contracts and clients of Compusearch when my contract expires with AOV. Each Conquest package is unique to the client because it is designed to suit their needs. This means there is no end to the learning process. I like the idea of working closely with different companies and helping them reach their customers and improve their performance. You get to see the results of your work, which I find rewarding and motivating. Ideally, I would like to end up at the Compusearch head office. However, I leave my future career goals open because things are ever changing and I may want to venture out to other challenges or opportunities.

◆

NOTES

1 *Source:* I.L.O., Taiwanese national statistics, *The Economist.*
2 *The Record* [Kitchener, Ont.], June 1, 1994, p. B5.
3 Canadian Ministry of Industry, Science, and Technology: Small Business Office, *Small Business in Canada: From Best Practice to Competitiveness* (Ottawa: Ministry of Supply, 1991).
4 Natasha Bacigalupo, "Wall Street Takes Shine to Canadian Graduates," *Financial Post*, June 4, 1994, p. 10.

3

JOB HUNTING

📁 **Profile:** *Tracy Albert, CFA*

- CURRENT POSITION
  Financial Analyst
  JRF Financial Consultants Ltd., Ottawa, Ontario
- EDUCATION
  Chartered Financial Analyst (CFA) Designation, 1993
  Canadian Securities Course, 1990
  Honours Bachelor of Commerce Degree,
  Finance, 1989, University of Ottawa

JRF Financial Consultants, the oldest investment-counselling firm in Ottawa, is a small company, which allows me to gain a broad range of experience in my job as an equity analyst. My work primarily involves studying a company's financial statements, analyzing its historical data and making forecasts of future earnings, dividends, and price levels. We also examine where the company is situated relative to its competitors in the same industry. We compare our forecasts of future stock price levels to the prices at which the company is trading presently in the market in order to determine whether the company is fairly valued. If we feel a company is undervalued in the market, we will consider adding it to a client's portfolio, assuming it meets the investment needs and risk-tolerance level of the client. If a company that we hold appears to be overvalued, we will consider selling it and replacing it with a company that has better prospects.

Our firm manages portfolios of institutions, charitable foundations and individuals. Although my primary function is to perform equity analysis of companies in various industries, I am also able to do fixed income analysis, cash flow analysis of client portfolios, as well as reporting to clients on the status of their portfolios. My Bachelor of Commerce Degree at the University of Ottawa allowed me to acquire some fundamental skills in the areas of financial statement analysis, statistical analysis, as well as hands-on experience with the computer. In my second year at school, I began working as a teaching assistant at the university. I helped a professor with courses that I had taken, and also was given the opportunity to assist him in graduate-level courses. This experience gave me additional practice in solving difficult problems, and helped me to develop a thought process that proved useful even in my other courses.

My relationship with this professor influenced my career path significantly. Through his extracurricular activities in the investment field in Ottawa, he had developed several contacts. When I graduated, he gave my name to an employer in the investment-counselling business in Ottawa. This led me to my job at JRF Financial Consultants. Shortly after I began working at JRF, I recognized the importance of continuing my education. In the first year I was with the firm, I completed the Canadian Securities Course offered by the Ontario Securities Commission. This course allowed me to gain practice at analyzing financial statements, and also taught me the terms and operations of the financial markets.

After completing the Securities Course, I registered for the Chartered Financial Analyst (CFA) designation. The CFA is a professional designation, recognized highly by firms in the investment field. This three-year course, beginning each December and ending each June, is an independent-study program, and encompasses seven courses: Ethics, Accounting, Economics, Equity Analysis, Fixed Income Analysis, Quantitative Analysis, and Portfolio Management. There is a final exam at the end of each year, which is a six-hour event covering all of the above subject areas.

Studying for the CFA designation allowed me to enhance my skills as an analyst. Perhaps more important, it taught me self-discipline, as well as the ability to juggle a full-time job and a very comprehensive course load. This experience is especially valuable since, to succeed as an analyst, one must be prepared to put in many hours of extra work. The CFA is highly recommended for students who wish to pursue a career in the investment field.

Company analysis is a dynamic process. It requires that I be on top of current events that could alter a company's fortunes. Now that I have completed my formal education, I can concentrate on the expansion of my knowledge of the companies that my firm studies. I also feel that it is important to learn from the masters in one's field. I can now spend some time reading the works of such investment masters as Peter Lynch and Warren Buffett. My plan is to keep working and learning to become well-versed in my area. My long-term goal is to become a partner in my firm.

◆

❙❙ *Introduction*

In this chapter we examine how to discover the job opportunities that are out there. No more than 15 percent of the jobs available to graduating students will be advertised in newspapers or your school placement office. Another given is that more than 80 percent of job hunters focus on this same 15 percent of available jobs. You may prefer the odds of being part of the 20 percent. By all means, use the newspapers and use your school placement office; just don't spend too high a proportion of your time and effort on these sources. Finding out about the hidden job market requires research, creativity, nerve, and tenacity. It also requires time. Treat the job-search process as a full-time course — your most important course. If you have already graduated, treat the job search as a full-time job. It requires discipline, organization and, above all, optimism.

▌▌ When Should I Start?

Right now! It does not matter whether you are a first-year student or are about to graduate, you should start now. Although it is not logical to take all of the steps outlined in this chapter in your first year, you can take some of them. We discuss networking in this chapter and you can give yourself a considerable head start by building your network right now. If you are only months away from graduation, it is time to go full speed into the job-search process.

I often hear a graduating student comment, "I think I'll start job hunting when I'm finished school — I'm too busy with mid-terms, exams, and projects to devote any time to job hunting." I understand the feeling, but if you take that attitude you are dead wrong for a variety of reasons. To some extent, spring is the hiring season. If you postpone your search, the competition has had first crack at the better jobs. You will also go through a period of time with little or no income and finally, and perhaps most importantly, you are putting yourself at a psychological disadvantage. You are unemployed and may be getting a bit desperate as the weeks and months go by. It is tough to stay optimistic under these conditions. From an employer's perspective, you might not have that all-important edge that a student about to graduate has.

▌▌ The Campaign

We want to launch a new soft drink onto the market. How will we ever persuade the public to buy our product? One consumer might be persuaded by the message contained in a TV ad. Another gets the jingle in her head while listening to the radio when driving home. Someone else had a taste in a mall and liked it, while another was attracted to the price reduction offered by the mailed coupons.

The company that designed this campaign realized that one promotional method was not enough. It had to use all of these strategies, plus others, because getting people to try the product was just a first step. It had to get people to decide this was their brand. I think the analogy is obvious. You, too, will have to use a variety of strategies to uncover job opportunities. It is too risky to rely on just one method.

Getting the recruiters to have a serious second look at you, or "rebuying," depends on your résumé and your performance in the job interview, both of which are covered later in the book. This chapter is directed toward the variety of techniques used in uncovering the hidden job market. Most successful job applicants use all the techniques.

▌▌ The Traps

STAY OPTIMISTIC

A word of caution! There are two traps waiting for you when you start this phase of the job-hunting process. First, you will have rejections. Most of you will have scores and very likely hundreds of rejections, either in the form of being ignored, receiving a "sorry . . . but" letter, getting a phone call, or being rejected in an interview. Of course, it is not easy, but it is a reality of the process. Do not let it knock down your optimism.

I recently talked to one of my former students who was determined to work for a major advertising agency. With a tenacity that surprised most of his peers, he was successful and today is very happy with his prospects in this company. This individual was not a scholarship student — he worked damned hard for everything he got. He had more than 100 rejections before he was through, but he ended up getting exactly what he wanted. I fully expect his career to follow a similar path. He had plenty of reasons to become despondent but he simply did not let it happen. This may seem like an extreme example, but your optimism will be tested. Hang tough!

DON'T BE TOO OPTIMISTIC

The other trap, ironically, is too much optimism. You have been successful in securing an interview and the interview went well. You become complacent and no longer work on uncovering other job opportunities; all activity has been put on hold while you wait for the offer, and the news that you have been rejected now comes as a shock. You have to start from scratch once again. It is simple — constantly feed more opportunities into the starting point of the process while you simultaneously go through the interviews your earlier efforts created for you. The greater the number of opportunities you uncover, the stronger the likelihood of a choice of good offers. It is not necessarily the top academic students that get the offers; it is the ones who constantly feed the process. Have a goal of securing, say, five fresh contacts each week.

Recently, a graduate had gone through a rigorous four-interview process with a potential employer. On the fourth interview, she was assured that she was the only candidate they were interested in, and after they cleared up a few details they would get back to her with an offer. She had already put a hold on her job-search activities and had even terminated the lease on her apartment. The company subsequently decided not to hire anybody and our student was left with no job, no prospects, and no apartment. Because she was not constantly feeding the job-search process she had to "restart the engine." Three difficult months later she did get a job.

▌▌ Making Contacts

As previously mentioned, there is no one best way — you should use all of the techniques about to be described. Having said that, the one technique that has become most important in recent years is networking. Networking is such a broad term that in this chapter we look at several of the techniques of networking. In fact, "making contacts" and "networking" are much the same thing. In networking, you are using your contacts.

Some of the material that follows will sound familiar. It should. The chapter on researching the job market covered many of the same techniques. Informational interviews, mock interviews and job shadowing are extremely useful in career planning, and are also a system of making contacts. When you engage in these and other activities, remember, you are accomplishing two tasks at once. The techniques of making contacts to be discussed are:

- Networking
- Family

- Former Employers
- Fellow Students
- Faculty
- School Projects
- Job Shadowing
- Mock Interviews
- Trade Shows
- International Exchange Programs

NETWORKING

Who should you approach when you start your networking? Everybody! This is a numbers game. The more people who know you are looking for a job, the better your chances. I know a graduating student who chatted with someone sitting in the next seat at a Blue Jays game, and it turned out this person was a sales manager for an industrial supplier. There were no job openings in his firm, but he thought that one of his colleagues might be looking for a salesperson. Names were exchanged, the student contacted the person, was able to mention the name of their mutual friend, an interview was set up, and two weeks later a good job offer was made and accepted.

The fact that the Jays won that afternoon may have helped set the mood, and I am not suggesting that every reader should head off to ball games armed with a stack of résumés. The point is, when you are in the market for a job, let people know. A valuable contact can be made in the most unlikely place. It has been said that through merely five levels of contacts you could be introduced to absolutely every living person in Canada. "Levels of contacts" means that if all your existing contacts shared their contacts, and those new contacts shared theirs, you would know all Canadians. I would not want to subject this homily to a statistical test, but it does make a point.

If you meet someone who can introduce you to someone and that person then will share their contacts, you can access many people and some of them are prospective employers.

When a student thinks of contacts, managers, department heads, and vice-presidents may come to mind. Certainly these people can be excellent contacts, but many students simply do not know anyone in that position. If you believe you have no contacts, examine the people that you do know. You may know a secretary who works for a particular company. This person, in turn, will be able to tell you who to contact in the organization. Perhaps they would be willing to speak to those people and let them know of your interest, and that you will be contacting them. If your contact would rather not make that approach, you can phone the appropriate person and say, "I was talking to Kim Johnson and she (or he) suggested that I contact you to discuss employment possibilities in your organization."

One of the more creative approaches to making contacts was described to me recently by one of my about-to-graduate students. He worked at a self-serve service centre on the Trans-Canada highway, which operated twenty-four hours a day. Business was often slow in the evening and he often chatted with customers. Being observant, he noticed that a high proportion of his customers used corporate credit cards. He was very quick to point out to them that he was going to be on the job market soon. He started collecting their business cards and then sending follow-up letters. He stepped up his campaign by bringing copies of his résumé to work and handing them out whenever a customer showed real interest. Again, the creative approach resulted in two job interviews and a dramatically increased network.

This example makes another critical point. Was this approach somewhat akin to hustling? Did it strike you as somewhat demeaning? It shouldn't. It was really clever. The business person would, in the majority of cases, drive away impressed by the student's inventiveness and aggressiveness. Not bad qualities for someone looking for a career in the business world.

Below is a list of some of the potential networks that you can use. It is usually best if you can have your acquaintance contact the person first, with you following up shortly afterwards. If that is not feasible, get the prospect's name and number and make the contact yourself. (See "The Phone Call" on page 96 of this chapter.)

FAMILY

People who may brag about how they got their job on their own and would not consider using their parents' influence were probably hired in the sixties or seventies when jobs were plentiful.

Besides, you are not using your family to get yourself a job, just a contact. If this ends up as a job, *you* got it! You may get an interview as a courtesy to your contact, but that is where the courtesy ends. The rest is up to you. If your parents or relatives have contacts, use them. Do not forget that you are focusing on the hidden job market.

FORMER EMPLOYERS

By now I am sure you have considered the prospects of actually working for your former employer. Let's assume that is not a viable option. Your employer, however, may have some contacts or advice on whom to contact. If they can make a contact for you, they can also mention something about your work habits. (Confirm that their comments will be positive.) If your former employers are business people, they will have a fairly wide circle of contacts that could prove to be valuable to you.

A former student of mine had worked for a supermarket as a cashier for two years. Her supervisor had suggested she apply to a particular manufacturer of houseware products. The supervisor contacted the manufacturer to let them know how good the employee was and to expect the call. This resulted in an interview and ultimately to a position in the accounting department.

FELLOW STUDENTS

I am sure your first reaction is surprise when I suggest that your fellow students can be part of your network. After all, you are competing against them, are you not? Sure, you are competing against them some of the time for some of the jobs, but more often than not you are in a position to help each other. On countless occasions, students have been hired and then their new employer indicates that they are "always in the market for a good prospect." They may even be more direct and ask the new employee to find out if other students might be interested in having an interview. Often when a company hires one person, that is an indication that they are in a hiring mode, and also that they like the graduates from your program.

There will be other circumstances in which a fellow student is not interested in a company after having an interview. This same job might be of interest to you, however. One student may be looking at multiple offers and when they accept one, the other companies are left still looking for someone. The other companies may have other prospects in the wings but those candidates were not the first choice and you might be preferred. No network is as mutually advantageous as is the student network. To receive, you will have to give. Of course, you protect your hot leads, but the chances are that if you are able to help a fellow student, at some point the favour will be returned. I cannot emphasize enough how well this network can operate if properly developed.

FACULTY

Student relationships with faculty vary dramatically from school to school. The number of students alone will cause this difference. Make sure your business faculty know you and know what you are looking for; also give them a copy or two of your résumé. Your professors have contacts and indeed may frequently get calls from industry asking them to select a few students for interviews. There is certainly an ethical question here. Some schools may want all employment contacts to go through their career placement office. It is pretty hard, however, when a company asks a professor to select a short list of candidates for interviews, to turn down the request.

As I write this chapter, I can see a résumé sitting on the corner of my desk. A student gave it to me a few days ago. He is interested in a sales/marketing position with a company involved in the production of building products, specifically wood products. He has a background in that industry from summer jobs. I know several people in the same industry and later today I will send copies of his résumé to these contacts. Two expressed a definite interest when I talked to them on the phone yesterday.

A colleague of mine had been spending a considerable amount of time helping one of her students with her résumé and career planning. The student just casually mentioned that she had worked for a hair-dressing salon before returning to school. When asked why it did not show up on her résumé she replied, "I didn't think that it was very relevant." My colleague helped her to change her résumé and directed her to several manufacturers of haircare products, where she ultimately got employment.

SCHOOL PROJECTS

Typically, a business student will have made several contacts in industry during their years at school — a business report or a research assignment required that you speak with someone in industry. That someone in industry is a contact. Establish a rapport and periodically keep in touch. I have some advice for first-year students. Start building contacts now. Every time you visit a company, take the attitude that you are being evaluated as a potential prospect even if graduation is four years away.

Not to be overlooked is the possibility of this contact resulting in summer employment, which could then lead to a full-time job at graduation. If your program of study does not take you into businesses, you can easily use other assignments as a lever to open the doors and talk to prospective employers. I have rarely had a year in which at least a couple of students did not end up working for the company for whom they did their market research project. These contacts give the companies a good look at you and you at them. You can impress them with your attitude, your work habits and your skills. It is very important, however, to nurture these contacts — do not let them forget you. At the appropriate time you can let them know you would like to discuss employment possibilities with them. If they have no opening, you will, of course, ask them for names of people that might be interested in you. This is the essence of networking.

JOB SHADOWING

Some schools may have "shadowing" as part of one of their courses, which gives you the opportunity to spend a day or two with someone in industry who is doing the type of work you would like to do. Even if it is not part of your course, simply phone up some companies and explain that you want to do some shadowing. It can be a great way of making another contact. Obviously, when you show up for your day of shadowing, you take the attitude that the company is having a very good look at you.

MOCK INTERVIEWS

A number of schools involve the students in mock interviews to give them practice at taking job interviews. Whether your school does this or not, you should set up some of these interviews. Although the prime purpose of a mock interview is to gain invaluable experience in being interviewed, with the interviewer critiquing your performance, this also represents another valuable contact. As mentioned earlier, it is also useful in career planning. Forget about the word "mock" when you go to this interview. Your research on the company, your dress and grooming, your résumé, and your conduct will be exactly as they would be for a "real" interview. Do not be surprised if these exercises turn out to be just that.

TRADE SHOWS

A rather unique school-associated activity that works very well for the marketing students at our school is a local trade show. A large food wholesaler holds a one-day trade show, which is attended by hundreds of food manufacturers and retail buyers. The sponsoring wholesaler uses our students as hosts and hostesses for the day. Not only does the wholesaler get a good look at the students, but the students have the opportunity to make a lot of contacts with a variety of food-processing companies. This one-day event has resulted in several job interviews and subsequent jobs.

INTERNATIONAL EXCHANGE PROGRAMS

Most universities and many colleges in Canada offer international student exchange programs in which students may work and/or study in another country. The period may range between one month and one year. Of course, participating in this type of program offers several obvious benefits, but it also offers students an excellent opportunity to make contacts. The largest of the exchange programs is AIESEC, which offers international job exchange programs that help students from foreign AIESEC locals get jobs here in exchange for Canadian students getting jobs in their countries. This organization operates in more than 500 universities in 69 countries! Any student completing an international exchange will return with several solid contacts, along with a far broader perspective on career planning.

▐▌ Getting Job Leads

With hard work and, yes, a bit of luck, some of the techniques of making contacts and building your network will eventually result in job leads and job interviews. In this section, more formal techniques of getting job leads are presented. The following sources of job leads are included:

- The School Placement Office
- Alumni
- Informational Sessions on Campus
- Newspaper Advertisements
- Trade and Professional Associations
- Trade Shows
- Employment Agencies

THE SCHOOL PLACEMENT OFFICE

Virtually all postsecondary institutions have a placement office. In my experience, they are universally staffed by hard-working, capable people. They offer a multitude of very valuable services; but for now, let's just focus on one aspect of the services provided — job leads. All placement offices on campus have contacts with industry. Through these contacts, companies may ask for résumés to be submitted along with the standardized application form. The companies may then short-list the applications and come on campus to interview those selected, or have the applicants come to their place of business. Do not overlook this source of job opportunity — it is quite easy.

However, as I mentioned before, you will find a lot of competition by going this route. I have, however, also heard companies complain about the lack of response to one of their own job postings. Many placement offices keep graduates on their mailing list for a period of time after they graduate. They may mail or phone you with recent listings, or if you still live in the area, you can go into their offices to check the listings. It is a good idea to check regularly for new listings and when the hiring season starts, to check daily.

ALUMNI

Unless you are a member of the first graduating class of your school, there are people out there who are predisposed to looking at you somewhat more favourably than applicants from other schools. Obviously, no business person is going to hire you simply because you share the same alma mater, but this common ground might get you an interview if all else is equal. It may be because they are familiar with the program of study and know it is good or it may simply be that they feel kindly toward the graduates of their alma mater.

The challenge is knowing how to tap into this resource. Many schools have a directory that lists alumni, giving the name of the firm, their title, and their address. That is a good start. Some schools offer an excellent "matching" service in which you fill out a detailed and standardized application form, usually kept in the alumni office. The University of Waterloo offers a computer-matched service in which the standard application is completed by the student and several résumés are placed in the file. When a request from an alumnus comes in, the job requirements are entered into the computer, which then attempts to match these requirements with the applicants' skills stored on a database. When there is a reasonable match, your résumé goes out.

You should check periodically to make sure the office is not running low on résumés. This is a great service. Be prepared for calls out of the blue from companies you have never heard of, telling you they found your résumé interesting and would like to interview you. If you get a job, or withdraw from the market, please let the alumni office and the school placement office know. They are usually overworked, so do not have them working on your file when it is not needed. You should also drop into their office and tell them about the job you got and how much you appreciated their help. Those are their real rewards.

📁 Profile: *Elizabeth Giardino*

- CURRENT POSITION

  Training & Recruitment Officer
  Human Resources Department
  Royal Bank of Canada
  Winnipeg, Manitoba

- EDUCATION

Bachelor of Arts, Administrative Studies, 1986, University of Winnipeg (completed while working)
Business Administration Diploma, 1982, Red River Community College

I have the unique distinction of being one of the only two management-level females with Manitoba Royal Bank in a job-share position. My partner and I each work three days per week, and have our own set of responsibilities. I held this position full time for three years before requesting a job-share arrangement, which allows for a better balance of work and family responsibilities.

Prior to the job-share arrangement, my responsibilities included: monitoring and evaluating the activities of twenty-five management trainees during their year-long training program; going on campus to recruit new graduates; providing classroom training on quality service and customer skills for our branch personnel; and such special projects as coordinating a career fair for 600 bankers and completing a study for senior management on mentoring.

My job-share arrangement is a great opportunity for both the bank and myself. I am now heading up a new training initiative that all our branch bankers will go through during the next two years. The bulk of my three days per week is spent in the classroom with branch managers and their staff. We work through understanding the bank's strategic direction, and implementing new approaches to meeting client needs. This project will keep me busy for the next two years.

I have always felt that ongoing learning is critical to one's success, and I think it was my own approach to education that made me a competitive candidate for my role. My college education gave me a chance to shine as a leader through various student activities as well as academic performance. The bank recruited me through the on-campus process, but as soon as I was working I started university evening courses and, eventually, completed my arts degree.

While progressing through various branch positions in the personal lending role, I completed a three-level certificate program offered by the Institute of Canadian Bankers. Next, I began the Chartered Financial Planner program, and at this point was offered the training and recruitment role in our head office.

Because the Human Resources Group is responsible for educating all our staff about career planning, I have considerable insight on the process and what I have to do to achieve my goals. I am, first, a banker and, second, a specialist in training, so I am looking to broaden my exposure. My next assignment will probably be a branch manager. I can then experience all that I have been training others to do.

I aspire to roles in general management, so I need client exposure and the chance to manage larger groups of people. Long-term goals include becoming manager of human resources, manager of a specialized function, or an area manager responsible for a number of branches. I am encouraged and supported by those around me that I can pursue my career objectives into senior management as well as balance work and family.

◆

_____

INFORMATIONAL SESSIONS ON CAMPUS

Some companies send representatives to campuses to talk about themselves, the types of careers available, and what they are looking for in their employees. Go to every one of these sessions. You will learn about the company and you will have opportunities to talk to company representatives, gaining some exposure for yourself and more contacts. Go to these sessions, having done some research so you can ask informed questions. A variation on the informational session is the "careers day" or "job fair" when a day may be set aside for several potential employers to set up booths, or merely to address the students, talking about careers in their particular industry. When you go to these sessions, take along copies of your résumé.

NEWSPAPER ADVERTISEMENTS

Remember the earlier comments about newspaper ads? Only a small minority of jobs are ever advertised, yet most job hunters use them as their prime source. A newspaper ad could easily draw over 100 applications. Furthermore, many of the companies that advertise in newspapers seem to be looking for a specific set of skills — skills you have not yet had an opportunity to develop.

That point aside, view the description of the desired candidate as the ideal — not what they are willing to take. Your part-time summer experience working in the accounting department of a local manufacturer will allow you to apply for the job that states "must have had at least two years accounting experience in the manufacturing sector."

You are light on experience, but you may be more current on some of the more recent software applications. Your covering letter will address the particular requirements of the advertised job and how you are a suitable prospect.

If you are looking for a job in another part of the country, go to a local store that carries out-of-town newspapers. Your school or public library may also carry them. Newspapers from other cities are usually a day late so you will be at a slight disadvantage. The only national newspaper is *The Globe and Mail*, and it is available the same day throughout most of Canada. Remember, a company that is advertising may be in a hiring mode. Even if the jobs advertised are not suitable, send a résumé and covering letter, indicating that you know the advertised positions are not what you are qualified for but that you are interested in . . . . . A number of trade journals have an employment section, so check these as well. Your library will have most of them. Although entry-level positions are not usually advertised in these trade publications, there are exceptions.

TRADE AND PROFESSIONAL ASSOCIATIONS

Trade associations and professional associations serve different purposes, but both can be useful in the job-search process. In the case of the professional associations, they can provide you with more information on careers in their field. Generally, they will be able to tell you what qualifications are needed to start a career in their profession. Figure 3.1 is a sampling of some professional associations in Canada. In many cases, each province has its own association. Any listing with an * is a national association. All others are provincial associations.

Figure 3.1. SAMPLE PROFESSIONAL ASSOCIATIONS IN CANADA

OCCUPATION	ASSOCIATION
Chartered Accountant	The Institute of Chartered Accountants of Ontario 69 Bloor Street East Toronto, Ontario M4W 1B3 Tel: (416) 962-1841 Toll-free: 1-800-387-0735

	Canadian Institute of Chartered Accountants* 277 Wellington Street West Toronto, Ontario M5V 3H2 Tel: (416) 977-3222 Fax: (416) 977-8585
Accountant	Certified General Accountants Association of Ontario 240 Eglinton Avenue East Toronto, Ontario M4P 1K8 Tel: (416) 322-6520 Toll-free: 1-800-668-1454 Certified General Accountants Association of Canada* 700 - 1188 Georgia Street West Vancouver, British Columbia V6E 4A2 Tel: (604) 669-3555
Computer Applications	Canadian Information Processing Society* 243 College Street, 5th floor Toronto, Ontario M5T 2Y1 Tel: (416) 593-4040 Data Processing Institute* P.O. Box 2458, Station D Ottawa, Ontario K1P 5W6
Data Processing Management	Data Processing Management Association of Canada* c/o Gendis Business Services 1370 Sony Place Winnipeg, Manitoba R3C 3C3 Tel: (204) 474-5200
Banking/Financial Analyst/ Financial Planning	The Canadian Bankers Association* The Exchange Tower, Suite 600 2 First Canadian Place Toronto, Ontario Tel: (416) 362-6092

	Trust Companies Association of Canada Inc.* 50 O'Conner Street Ottawa, Ontario KIP 6L2 Tel: (613) 563-3205 Trust Companies Institute 35 Bay Street, Suite 205 Toronto, Ontario M5H 2O3 Tel: (416) 364-1210
Hotel, Restaurant, and Hospitality Management	The Ontario Hotel and Motel Association 6725 Airport Road, Suite 102 Mississauga, Ontario L4V IV2 Tel: (416) 672-9141 Canadian Restaurant and Food Services Association* 80 Bloor Street West Toronto, Ontario M5S 2BI Tel: (416) 923-8416 Canadian Hospitality Foundation* 80 Bloor Street West, #120 Toronto, Ontario M5S 2VI Tel: (416) 923-8416 Canadian Hospitality Institute* 390 Queen's Quay West, #2012 Toronto, Ontario M5V 3A6 Tel: (416) 260-1371
Human Resources Management	Human Resources Professionals Association of Ontario 2 Bloor Street West, Suite 600 Toronto, Ontario M4W 3E2 Tel: (416) 923-2324 Toll-free: 1-800-387-1311

	Canadian Association of Human Resource Systems Professionals Inc.* 181 University Avenue, #1202 Toronto, Ontario M5H 3M7 Tel: (416) 367-2567
Life Insurance/Financial Planning	Life Underwriters Association of Canada* 41 Lesmill Road Don Mills, Ontario M3B 2T3 Tel: (416) 444-5251
Real Estate Sales	The Ontario Real Estate Commission 99 Duncan Mills Road Don Mills, Ontario M3B 1Z2 Tel: (416) 445-9910 The Canadian Real Estate Association* Tower A, #2100, 320 Queen Street Ottawa, Ontario K1R 5A3 Tel: (613) 234-3372 Fax: (613) 234-2567
Stockbroker/Security Advisor/ Investment and Counsellor	Investment Dealers Association of Canada* 33 Yonge Street Toronto, Ontario M5E 1E5 Tel: (416) 364-6133
Public Service	The Public Service Commission* 171 Slater Street Ottawa, Ontario K1A 0M7 Tel: (613) 996-8436

In addition to these professional associations, the multitude of trade associations can provide you with some useful information as well. Trade associations are typically organized around a particular industry, for example, The Canadian Pharmaceutical Manufacturers Association. You can get from them a listing of all their member companies and often some names of contact persons within those companies. The

Directory of Trade and Professional Associations is the best source for a listing of these associations in Canada.

Another useful group of associations is the student chapters of professional associations on your own campus. By all means, join them and play an active role in their activities. Among the many benefits you can derive from being a member is developing contacts. If your major area of interest is marketing, join the marketing club on campus. Examples of the clubs/associations available at a variety of schools across Canada are:

- Commerce Society
- Entrepreneurs Society
- Small Business Club
- Toastmasters
- Business Student Association
- Accounting Club
- Marketing Club

Although the purposes of these clubs vary, most have good speakers. You will enhance what you are learning in your business courses and you will also be able to develop important contacts in industry by participating. These groups are respected by business, as is illustrated by the University of Alberta Business Student Representative. The student representatives of this group become members of the Edmonton Chamber of Commerce.

TRADE SHOWS

Just imagine, a couple of hundred potential employers all collected together under one roof! Are you interested in the computer industry, the sporting-goods industry, the giftware industry? These industries, and hundreds of others, hold trade shows each year. Some are very easy to get into and others are more restricted. Students can often get in as part of a school project. Your professor may be able to help. If you are still having trouble, approach a retailer that might be attending and ask if you can accompany them.

Travel with a stack of résumés. Approach the company representatives, ask about the product/service, and let them know how interested you are in their organization. If you are not making progress, try to get the name of a contact person in that company. Phone up a couple of days later and say, "I was talking to Ms. Wilson at the gift show last week and I'd like an opportunity to discuss employment possibilities with your organization. I find your industry very interesting." With this approach, you have certainly set yourself apart from any other "cold" caller. You have shown your interest by attending their trade show, you have talked to someone in their organization, and you have shown you are aggressive and resourceful, both sterling qualities for the nineties.

Various trade show directories, your local convention centre, and the larger hotels all have listings of upcoming trade shows. Contact a company in the industry that interests you and ask them in which trade shows they will be participating.

Every Tuesday, Thursday, and Friday, *The Globe and Mail* publishes the "Globe Comm — The National Event Hotline." This is a listing of upcoming trade and consumer shows across Canada and internationally. It provides a toll-free number (1-800-665-3555) and a four-digit code for each of the listed trade shows, which provides a recorded message giving additional information on the show. Just glancing at today's "Globe-Comm," I see it is listing an "Industrial Expo — New Brunswick" trade show in Saint John. The Retail Council's Annual Conference slated for next week has as its theme "Join the Retail Revolution," and will be held in Toronto, while another trade show and conference has as its theme "Mexico — The New Trade Frontier." Those are but three examples of the nineteen listed trade shows.

Trade shows differ in format, but almost all include exhibits by suppliers of products and/or services. Here is where you can make contacts. Some of these shows offer reduced prices for students or group rates for a whole class. As well as exhibiting, most conferences have guest speakers. Business trends and opportunities is often the common thread running through the presentations at these conferences. What valuable information for someone engaged in career planning!

Consumer shows tend not to provide a very conducive environment to accomplish what you want. They are usually very crowded and the people in the booth may not be the ideal contacts and probably have little time to talk to you. That aside, approaching them might provide you with a contact.

EMPLOYMENT AGENCIES

These agencies may fill a very important role in your job search in about five years' time. Although some graduates may get jobs by using the services of employment agencies, the agencies tend to deal with applicants who have had a few years' experience. In a tight economy, potential employers are reluctant to pay a fee to an employment agency for a recent graduate. They know that their own recruiting process can gain them a good selection of applicants from which they can short-list. Other companies, and they are growing in number, will not recruit. They are interested in only those students aggressive enough to chase after them. If, however, you have a few years' experience, or you have graduated from a co-op program that gave you good experience, a placement agency could be a useful addition to your job-hunting campaign.

Bear in mind that employment agencies are focused on fulfilling the need of the employer, not the employee — after all the employer pays the fee. If you are asked to pay a fee or take a course that they offer, walk out. The vast majority of placement agencies are ethical and, as mentioned earlier, can be helpful in getting you a job later on in your career.

"Head hunters" are even more focused than the employment agencies. They are looking for a very specific set of skills and considerable experience. Again, they may play a role in your job-hunting strategy in about five years.

▌▌ Getting the Interview

A passive approach to getting the interview is doomed to failure. Just sending off a résumé to a prospective employer and hoping for a phone call is, for the most part, a waste of time, paper, and postage. Getting an interview is a process — a process you must manage.

You have done most of the hard work already. Now you are about to tackle the psychologically difficult part of the process — lining up the interview. As discussed under the "Traps" section of this chapter, rejection is part of this process. If you cannot get an interview with a particular company, do not reprove yourself. You are looking for one job, and to get it you will approach dozens or, in some cases, hundreds of companies. A lot of approaches will end in refusal; it is normal and it is not a reflection on yourself. You will have to take a lot of shots on net before one goes in, and there is certainly no one right way to try to get an interview.

In this section we examine making the initial approach by letter or fax, by phone, in person, and a blend of all of these techniques. Regardless of the technique used, always have the name and title of the person you want to contact. A letter addressed to "Dear Sir/Madam" or "Dear Office Manager" is destined for the waste basket; after all, they do not have anybody with that name working there.

▌▌ The Effective Letter

Although a personal approach is often better, sheer numbers and distance often make it impractical, leaving the letter accompanying your résumé as the only choice. Please review "The Covering Letter" in Chapter 4. Below is a brief summary of the points covered in that section.

If your letter is in response to an advertisement, tailor the letter to that ad. If the ad mentioned that familiarity with Harvard Graphics or Mail Merge would be an asset, and you are familiar with both systems, state that in your covering letter. Even if your résumé has that same information, point it out anyway.

In your letter, highlight the points of your résumé that you believe would be of particular interest to that company. If you can add a comment or two in your letter, you will set yourself apart from the other one hundred responses they received.

Do not make the mistake of reading the ad and setting it aside for a week while you research the company's background. When you see the ad, research the company that day and send your letter and résumé off immediately. If practical, hand-deliver your résumé.

If a name is not given in the ad, phone the company and find out who your response should be addressed to. Mail or fax? A faxed letter and résumé get there faster and some companies believe it to be more businesslike. With a fax, you will, of course, lose the impact of your good bond paper and laser-printed copy.

The letter that accompanies an unsolicited résumé has a few differences. You do not have the required qualifications outlined for you in an ad, so your letter will refer to some of your more generic skills. You will also have had an opportunity to do more research on the company and your letter should reflect this. Although you may be sending out hundreds of letters and résumés, the letters must not sound like a form letter — tailor each one to each company. All mailed-out résumés should be followed up by a phone call. Your letter will have indicated that you will be contacting them to set up a time for an interview. Think positively.

▌▌ The Phone Call

Phoning is faster — it gives you an opportunity to deal with objections and you cannot be ignored the way your mailed résumé might be. Before you phone, research the company, know why you are interested in them, and know why they should be interested in you. Remember the purpose of the call; it is not to get a job, but it is to get an interview.

Your first challenge is to get past the gate-keeper or receptionist/secretary. You will, of course, have the name of the person you want to talk to. A firm "I'd like to speak to Ms. Robertson" is infinitely better than saying, "Who should I speak to about a job interview?"

Try to avoid the human resources department. Speak directly to the person who would be your boss if you were to be hired. This is an end run but it can put you ahead of the pack. Assume the moment of truth has arrived and you are now speaking to the right person. The opening comment is very important. You identify yourself, let her know you want to discuss employment opportunities and why you are particularly interested in her organization. The reasons, of course, will have come from your research on the company. Now it is time to be quiet. No long opening speeches. It is quite possible you have caught her interest. If her response does show interest (I do not mean she wants to book an interview time), then you can tell her a bit more about yourself, obviously those strong points you emphasized on your résumé and a bit more on what you know about the company.

You should now take the next logical step and ask when would be a good time to set up an interview. The moment you get a positive response on an interview and the time and place are set, thank her and get off the phone. Do not talk yourself out of anything.

A very common response will be, "We don't need anybody at this time" or one of a dozen variations of this statement. This is NOT A NO.

Seize the moment and respond with, "I'm still very interested in your organization and would like an opportunity to explore potential employment opportunities for the future. Could we set up a time when we could discuss this?"

If this does not work, ask if there is someone else in the company that might be interested in you. Get that person's name and phone them. You can now say, "I was just talking to Ms. Robertson and she suggested that I call you regarding employment." If Ms. Robertson did not give you a name of someone in the organization, perhaps she could give you the name of someone in the same industry that might be interested.

If all of these probes fail, tell her you are going to send a résumé so that she can keep it on file. Send it and phone about a week later to make sure she got it. At that time you might ask whether your qualifications are suitable for that company. If so, indicate that you will be calling back periodically to see if any opportunities have developed. You will, of course, do just that. This is an aggressive approach but in business, aggressiveness is a strength, not a weakness.

You may have to remind yourself that your aggressiveness will rarely offend, and in the majority of cases, it will make you a person they are almost afraid to ignore.

In many cases you will be phoning someone whose name you got from a contact. As already stated, networking can give you a long list of names. Any time you call and can mention a contact's name, getting the attention of a prospective employer is easier.

Making these "cold calls" by phone is not easy. Most of us have to muster our courage before making the call. It is a good idea to prepare a written script to help you through the first thirty seconds of the call, when you have to make a good impression. Try taping this script so you can hear how you sound, and do several "takes" until you are satisfied.

▌▌ Follow-Up

Start a file on every company you contact, whether by mail or by phone. Date, name, title and address of all contacts, a précis of any conversation, and a date for follow-up should be entered into this file. It takes organization and diligence during this phase of the job search.

▮▮ Conclusion

As you can now see, the strategy you use in job hunting determines how many interviews you get. Although your interviewing techniques ultimately determine your success, there is a definite quantitative aspect to job hunting. Most jobs are won by being resourceful and aggressive. You are looking at a process that will take a lot of time and organization. You cannot let yourself get down simply because you have had a lot of refusals. If only one out of every twenty-five contacts results in a quality job interview, that does not represent failure. Develop a couple of hundred contacts so you will have lots of interesting possibilities. Use all of the techniques discussed in this chapter. You will be surprised at how quickly your contact list will grow.

📁 Profile: *Robert Bellisle*

- **CURRENT POSITION**

  Account Representative
  Eastern Canada Plate and Structurals Division
  Algoma Steel Inc.
  Mississauga, Ontario

- **EDUCATION**

Bachelor of Commerce, Marketing, Managerial Law (Minor), 1993, Concordia University

As an account representative at Algoma Steel, my duties involve providing constant service to customers via telephone and data communication. Daily duties include booking, modifying, and expediting orders as well as responding to any customer inquiries on such things as product range, chemical or physical grades and tolerances of products, and delivery lead times. As a member of the Eastern Canada Plate and Structurals division, my task is to service the Quebec market for a customer base ranging from resale to construction.

In addition to my primary task as account representative, I also serve as the EPU representative for the Plate and Structurals' commercial division. As an employee participation unit representative, my responsibilities are to assist fellow employees with any ideas or issues, investigate and provide effective feedback to employees on these issues, as well as making "go"/"no-go" decisions on budgetary spending within my designated unit.

During my four years at Concordia University, I took a balanced load of courses covering both the theoretical and application sides of business. In my core technical courses such as Accounting, Finance and Decision Sciences, I learned what financial impact a company's marketing strategies have on its balance sheet and how these strategies can affect the company's financial position. In courses that lent themselves to the case-study method, I was asked to prepare formal presentations on marketing strategies, which my classmates and I developed based on the information provided in the case. These courses were a key tool in preparing me for the type of formal presentations and strategic decisions I make now.

After graduating, I approached my job hunt using the skills that I had acquired through the case-study method. I first developed my mission statement, which not only encompassed my end goal (i.e., finding a job), but also some personal values that would provide guidelines during my career. Focusing on these values, I began to analyze the job market. I quickly realized that though I had excellent interpersonal skills, my contacts in the business community were scarce. So I began attending seminars, dinners, cocktails, and sending résumés to organizations that I thought blended well with my mission statement.

I followed up my résumés with either a proactive phone call or an in-person visit, depending, of course, on the geographical location of the company. I also approached the university's on-campus employment centre for some help. I attended their seminars and applied for various positions through the placement centre. It was through this centre that I landed my job at Algoma Steel.

My long-term career goal is one that is based not only on social and economic status and growth, but also on my impact with people on a personal and psychological level. I would like to become the general manager for the Plate and Structurals division one day, but more importantly, I want to contribute to the growth of positive communication within the organization. My current responsibilities as an EPU representative will serve as the foundation for building this environment.

RÉSUMÉS

📁 **Profile:** *Sherry Shaw-Froggatt*

- CURRENT POSITION

  Manager, Advertising and Creative Services
  Alberta Motor Association (AMA)
  Edmonton, Alberta

- EDUCATION

  Certified Advertising Agency Practitioner,
  Institute of Canadian Advertising, 1990
  Business Administration Diploma, Marketing
  Management, 1985, Northern Alberta Institute
  of Technology

As Manager of Advertising and Creative Services at Alberta Motor Association, CAA, my objective is to effectively manage the department to meet the needs of our internal clients. I juggle a number of responsibilities, some of which include developing, administering, and managing the systems/processes needed to flow work through the department; acting as Account Director for all internal client accounts; planning strategies, and purchasing media; and managing all projects to meet deadlines, and client demands.

Looking back, I am glad that I chose NAIT. For each job I have held since graduation, NAIT has played a key role. The Marketing program has a practical approach, and the second-year course projects provide an opportunity to become directly involved in the industry. My NAIT background provided leverage and credibility with an organization as large as the *Edmonton Journal*. I talk to many advertising hopefuls and always recommend NAIT.

Through NAIT's advertising project I made my first contact in the industry I love. The president of one of Alberta's largest ad agencies spoke at our Awards Evening. His words were, "If you want to work in advertising, start in a small-town newspaper." I took his advice, and for two years, I not only sold and designed ads for a small weekly newspaper, but I was also responsible for typesetting, layout, pasteup, editorial, photography, and reporting.

When I decided it was time to apply for a position in an advertising agency, I sent my résumé to the same president who had spoken at our Awards Evening, and who had so far guided my career. In my letter, I challenged him to back up his advice by hiring me, and he did!

In 1990, I worked with the *Edmonton Journal* as an advertising representative. After leaving the *Edmonton Journal*, I started my my own marketing consulting business called Leap Frog Marketing, developing strategies, media buying, and creative development for various clients. However, after a brief stint with my own business, I was once again lured back to the paid work force and was offered a job as the Manager of Advertising and Creative Services for the Alberta Motor Association (AMA).

Over the years, I have tried to help students by giving talks at NAIT on creative job hunting. I encourage students to advertise themselves "to the max" by offering potential employers a test drive: work for free to get a foot in the door. If you can't seem to get your foot in the door, try this: send a print of your footprint with the copy, "Help a marketing grad get her foot in the door." Follow up with your résumé, and then call and ask, "Has Ms. Johnson received my foot in the mail?" I got three interviews for positions that were not even advertised!

Competition is tough in the job market. Over the years, I've learned to see myself as the product, the résumé as my greatest sales tool, and the interview as the sales pitch. Considering the golden rule of sales, which is 90 percent preparation and 10 percent presentation, your cover letter and résumé must be tailored to the company, and more importantly, to the person who decides which résumés to consider. Preparing a résumé is a laborious and often stressful process; after all, it is your life condensed to two 8½ x 11 sheets, besides your covering letter. Every covering letter should entice the reader to continue, like a great mystery, to the next page. Always highlight something from your résumé that directly ties in with the company's overall corporate image or strategy or mission statement. If none of this is available, use a line directly from the position description.

My future goal is to head my own advertising agency on a larger scale with time for golf. Running my own business and now working at AMA have put me in a management position where I have the opportunity to affect someone else's future. What do I look for in a résumé? Humour and creativity, involvement in extracurricular activities, a résumé that reaches out and grabs me by the collar and says, "Yah gotta meet this person" — and absolutely no typos.

◆

▮▮ *Introduction*

Think back to the last term paper you prepared. What a lot of work it was! You had to research, make rough notes, prepare an outline, decide on the order of the information you were going to present, prepare a rough draft, refine, prepare another draft, refine until you believed you had a good report. You may have had a friend read it, which resulted in further refinement. Your proofreader read it very carefully and then you finally submitted it by the assigned date. This whole process may have taken several weeks, or even months, depending on the length and complexity of the assignment. In time, your professor returned your report with critical comments pointing out its strengths, or quite possibly, its deficiencies.

It is a good idea to view your preparation of a résumé in the same light. You will have to do research; you will prepare several drafts with each one resulting in further refinements, and have other people critically evaluate it before you have a finished product. You can see that there are a number of similarities between a comprehensive school project and preparing a résumé. It is equally important to understand the differences between the two. The most obvious difference is length. A résumé may be one or two pages, while a report may range from ten to forty pages. That makes the résumé more difficult, not less. You must be incredibly efficient with your words, losing none of the information you wish to communicate. The other major difference is that the school report is marked and handed back so you can see where you must improve the next time. Mistakes on résumés mean they are tossed out without a second thought and you will never know why.

▮▮ Understanding a Résumé

WHAT IS A RÉSUMÉ?

A résumé is a document that shows the reader what you can do, based on what you have done. In essence, you are telling the reader, "I have supervised people in my part-time job at the service station; therefore I can supervise people for your organization." "I was the chair for the fund-raising campaign on campus; therefore I have leadership skills I can bring to your organization." "I financed 80 percent of my education; therefore I know how to work hard and sacrifice." "I was in the top 10 percent of my class; therefore I have some mental agility and can learn new job demands quickly." These and countless other statements, although certainly not worded as I have just expressed them, are what you must communicate to the reader. Remember the earlier comments on company recruiters looking at the bottom line? They want to know what you can do now, not just what you will be able to do for the organization in a few years. Your résumé had better show them this.

WHAT IS THE PURPOSE OF A RÉSUMÉ?

That is easy — to get you the interview. The résumé will not get you a job. You will get the job by what takes place in the interview and its follow-up. Stated negatively and realistically, your résumé, if only average or worse, will prevent you from getting the interview.

DO I REALLY NEED A RÉSUMÉ?

Obviously the answer is yes. If you are fortunate enough to have tentatively lined up a job upon graduation, you still need the résumé. Perhaps you worked for a company part time and you were told you would be hired full time upon graduation. Your supervisor probably added, "Drop in for a chat in April and we'll discuss the details." Treat this as you would any other selection process by having a well-prepared résumé. An application form is not a substitute for a résumé. Actually, a résumé makes filling out an application form much easier.

WHEN SHOULD I PREPARE IT?

Another easy question — now. If you are a first-year student, it is time to start work on your résumé. You are, or will be, looking for part-time or summer employment. There are a lot of students chasing a diminishing supply of jobs. A good résumé can give you that edge. In the long term, a more important advantage of preparing a résumé a year or more before graduation is that you will have an opportunity to refine it over a period of time. I do not mean just adding additional job experience each year, but truly refining it. The more time you have for this process, the better the résumé. If you are in your graduation year, it is critical that you immediately learn the process of preparing a résumé. Ideally, you should have the finished product about four months before graduation. I have often seen panic-stricken students scrambling to prepare a résumé upon hearing that some companies are coming on campus for job interviews in a week's time, and they do not have their résumés done. The first product usually reflects that haste.

Another good reason to have a résumé prepared well before graduation is to be ready to take advantage of situations that develop suddenly. You meet someone in business during a school project and they show interest in you. What a perfect time to give them a copy of your résumé!

Perhaps you are a first- or second-year student and your professor brings a guest speaker to the class. You enjoy the presentation and the prospects of working for that company are exciting. You talk to the visitor after class, showing your interest, and ask if you can give or send a résumé to them. By having the résumé ready, you set yourself apart from the other students who share your enthusiasm, but not your preparedness.

WHAT ELSE CAN A GOOD RÉSUMÉ DO FOR ME?

The process of preparing a résumé, combined with a detailed personal inventory-taking process, also prepares you for the interview. You know who you are and what skills you have to offer and exactly where you gained those skills. You are in a far better position to discuss all your assets with the interviewer. Nothing is as frustrating as realizing after the interview that you missed discussing one of your strong points.

WHY IS THE RÉSUMÉ SO IMPORTANT?

Perhaps this question should read, "Why is having an excellent résumé so important?" After all, are they not pretty standard? If you were preparing advertising copy, you would put yourself in the position of the reader or viewer of your ad. A résumé is the same thing. You are selling something — yourself — to the reader. Put yourself in the shoes of the reader. Your résumé may be one of hundreds of résumés. Just as an advertisement has to stand out against hundreds of other ads, so does your résumé. Will they carefully read and study your résumé? Not a chance. Do you carefully read or listen to advertising? No, it has to grab you. Recruiters and human-resource personnel may spend thirty seconds, or less, glancing at one résumé. Yours simply must stand out. Just as you hold a remote control to use when an advertisement is boring when you watch TV, the résumé reader has a mental remote control. Producing this stand-out résumé is a daunting task. But it is a sad or encouraging fact — depending on one's perspective — that many résumés are not well prepared, reducing the level of competition.

HOW LONG SHOULD A RÉSUMÉ BE?

There is considerable debate on length. Some people say a graduating student should be able to get it all down on one page. Perhaps you may have had some relevant experiences you simply cannot condense into one page. A crowded page just does not invite one to read it. For many students, two pages would be an acceptable length. Beyond two pages is too long. Even for someone in the business world with ten years of experience, the résumé would not likely exceed two pages. Remember, the reader may spend a mere thirty seconds looking at it.

WHAT HAPPENS WHEN A COMPANY RECEIVES A RÉSUMÉ?

What happens with a résumé varies considerably with the size of the company. A medium-to-large company may have the human-resources department screen résumés to short-list them to twenty promising candidates. They may then be forwarded to the manager who will be supervising the person upon employment. The manager may further screen the résumés to short-list them down to five or six. Smaller companies may not have this intermediate step in the human-resources department. While the above process is far from standard, one part of it is — screening. The readers of the résumés are not looking for the right candidate nearly as much as they are looking for ways to screen, that is, eliminate unsuitable résumés. Remember, at this point you do not exist in the potential employer's eyes, only your résumé does. If that potential employer can spot a spelling mistake, an uninviting layout, confusing communication, or less-than-precise wording in the thirty seconds dedicated to your résumé, it quickly goes in the do-not-interview pile.

▌▌ Common Mistakes in a Résumé

Below is a list of some of the most common mistakes found in résumés.

• *Too long and/or too wordy*

Remember the thirty-seconds rule! You must express yourself clearly and concisely. You will have an opportunity to expand upon your points in an interview. If your résumé is not concise, it might suggest an inability to think concisely.

• *Unattractive*

Is the content not more important than the package? What is more important in a car, the styling or the transmission? Treat each with equal importance. With desk-top publishing readily available, you can convey to the reader that you are an organized person by having a well-laid-out and organized résumé.

- *Too different from the norm*

This can be a tough call. If you graduated in graphic arts or fashion design, a highly creative, unusual résumé might work well. If you are graduating from a business program and entering the business world, which is a fairly conservative environment, a more standard form is appropriate. It is not entirely accurate, however, to view the business world as a homogeneous entity. In advertising, more creativity in a résumé is indicated than if you were applying to an accounting firm. It can be a fine balancing act between making your résumé stand out and staying within the relatively conservative boundaries of acceptability. This subject is discussed in some detail under "Packaging the Résumé."

- *Too much emphasis on income*

For a graduating student, any mention of either past, current, or future salary expectations is a mistake. This is particularly true in the recessionary nineties when salary gains are typically modest or nonexistent. You might convey the image of being money hungry. The subject of past salary and future expectations will come up during the interview, a process in which you might not participate if your first exposure to a potential employer includes salary demands.

- *Including photographs and personal information*

It is illegal for a potential employer to ask for a photograph or personal information. To voluntarily include this information is a badly dated practice. Occasionally, subtle racism or other forms of discrimination resulted from the inclusion of such details. Height, weight, marital status, and birth date should not be part of any résumé. At one time, some employers believed that a married candidate might be more stable than a single one. However, few professional recruiters have believed this for many years.

- *Small errors*

Remember the discussion of how an employer uses a résumé? It is a screening device and what better or easier way to reduce the pile of résumés than simply tossing those with spelling, grammatical, or typographical errors.

🗂 Profile: *Julie Ferguson*

- CURRENT POSITION

  Market Researcher
  Hewlett Packard Company
  Brussels, Belgium

- EDUCATION

  Bachelor of Arts, Economics, 1994,
  University of New Brunswick

I have been accepted to work in Belgium for a year as a market researcher for Hewlett Packard. This opportunity came about because of my involvement at UNB in AIESEC, an international organization committed to the development of students and to promoting internationalism. AIESEC runs an international traineeship exchange program between students and companies in its seventy-eight member countries and matches companies to students with the specified qualifications.

Before I knew that I was accepted to go to Belgium, I had applied for a summer position as assistant coordinator of a brand new program at UNB called Transition to Employment. Although I had no actual work experience in the field of program development, my involvement with AIESEC really helped me get the job, as did the great references that I got from the people that I worked for in my past summer jobs. One of my references did not wait to be called. He knew the person who was in charge of hiring and called to endorse my application. I think it was that call that got me the interview for this summer position.

I also got help in my preparation for this interview from the UNB Student Placement Service. They provided me with videos on successful interview tips. They also offer workshops on developing an effective résumé. The important thing to remember about résumés is that they just get you in the door. If your résumé is not good, you will not even get the chance to convince the employer that you could do a good job. I am always careful to look over my résumé before applying for a job to ensure that I have brought out all the points of the position requirements. Often, this means adjusting my résumé to the specific job. I also never use the same cover letter. I do some research on the company, and try to relate my experience and skills to the qualifications the job requires.

I am just beginning to realize that every job a student holds becomes important when they leave university to look for permanent work. Employers like to see that you have some experience. If you find it difficult to get summer or during-school jobs in your field, volunteer your services — the experience is just as good and will help you to develop the skills you need to get ahead in the career you choose. One of the ways I developed business experience and practical skills was by being involved with AIESEC.

As president of AIESEC, I worked closely with our advisory board made up of people from the university and business community. I now have a network of people who can act as references for me. In my position as regional manager, I organized a regional training conference in which internal and external trainers spoke to the members about marketing, public relations, and working as a team.

Because of AIESEC, I now have organization and leadership skills that look excellent on my résumé. They also happen to be important criteria that many employers look for in deciding who to interview for a position. Sure, it gets to be a lot of work, and can sometimes be frustrating. But I know that there will be thousands of Business and Commerce graduates trying to get jobs this year. What do I have on my résumé that distinguishes me from all the others and helps to put me into the "yes" pile?

Working on the Transition to Employment program all summer helped me to decide that I would like to have a career that involves project development, training and public relations work, perhaps in the personnel, development, marketing, or public relations departments of a company. When I return from Belgium, I also plan to begin marketing an interactive training seminar that a friend and I developed, which is designed to help students to recognize the importance of career planning, and deal with some of the obstacles that lie ahead of them.

◆

▮▮ Preparing Your Résumé Worksheets

You are now ready to start writing. Not your résumé; that will come later, but rather some worksheets for each section of the résumé. From these completed work sheets, you will have all the information you need to prepare your first draft of the résumé. Beginning on page 125, you can find descriptions of various styles of résumés, but regardless of what style you select, the worksheet approach is very useful. Much of the information in these worksheets will not make it onto the résumé but, just as in film production, a major key to success is editing.

You have already completed much of your background work for preparing the worksheets. You completed a self-assessment chart at the start of your career-planning process, and from that you identified your transferable skills and abilities. These are the same skills and abilities that will appear on your résumé. They will be edited and written in a very precise form, but they will be there.

Throughout this book the process of career planning is emphasized. To prepare a résumé without first completing a self-assessment is like preparing an advertising campaign without knowing the product's selling features or differential advantages.

I would suggest setting up worksheets using the following headings:

A.   Career Objectives
B.   Highlights of Qualifications
C.   Education History
D.   Additional Training/Courses
E.   Extracurricular Activities
F.   Employment History
G.   Volunteer Experience
H.   Outside Interests
I.   References

Sample worksheets are provided in Figure 4.1 at the end of this section. I am not suggesting that all of these headings will actually appear on the résumé, but most likely some of the information from these sections will. As well, the chronology of these headings does not necessarily suggest the order in which the edited information will appear in the résumé.

CAREER OBJECTIVES

You may decide not to include this section in your final résumé, but it is essential that you at least draft a career-objective statement. The problems in preparing a career-objective statement are twofold. The statement may be too focused — "An entry level position in the accounting department of a life insurance company" is fine, but why restrict your- self to life insurance? The other extreme could read something like "An interesting position in the sales and marketing field." That statement is so broad as to be meaningless. You would be projecting yourself as indecisive and uncertain.

To strike an acceptable middle position between these extremes is a challenge. For that reason, many candidates elect not to include that section on the résumé, and instead, include a widely focused job-objective statement with a covering letter directed toward a specific company. Having your résumé on disk eases the process of changing the job objective, depending on the company to which you are sending your résumé.

Any job-objective statement should include what type of job you want, what type of organization you want to work for, and at what level you want to start.

For example, you may want to work in the human-resources depart-ment (where) in the health-care industry (for whom) in an entry-level position (at what level). Restated, your job objective could read: An entry-level position in the human-resources department for an organi-zation in the health-care field.

Other examples:

1. An assistant purchasing agent for a major manufacturer.
2. An assistant product manager for a manufacturer of consumer packaged goods.
3. A production scheduler for a producer of food products.
4. An inside salesperson leading to outside sales for a manufacturer of industrial equipment.

An important ingredient of a well-prepared job-objective statement is how it relates to the transferable skills you are offering the potential employer. Either your education and training, or your previous work experience must validate your job objective. Note that these statements generally address the position you are looking for now, not in the long term. It is acceptable (as in example 4) to indicate what the job might lead to.

HIGHLIGHTS OF QUALIFICATIONS

This optional section is a kind of mini-résumé giving the reader a snapshot of your particular strengths. When people who have the responsibility of wading through stacks of résumés see an increasing number arriving almost daily, they cut down the amount of time they spend on each one. We have repeatedly mentioned the thirty-seconds time-frame, which suggests the importance of a summary statement. This section demonstrates that you are self-assured and exactly the right person for the job. A well-prepared summary invites the reader to continue going through the résumé. Some information that you might include in this section would be:

1. The quality and quantity of relevant experience
2. Educational highlights, including two or three particularly relevant courses
3. Educational achievements such as your standing in your class and awards
4. An exceptional skill or ability.

For example:

"Three years part time in retail sales and four times winner of salesperson of the month."
"Consistently in top quarter of my class."
"Courses in retail merchandising, selling techniques, and retail management."
"Self-directed and able to motivate others."

Too often, the summary of qualifications becomes a dumping ground of claims that are unsubstantiated. If you state that you have "strong oral presentation skills" you had better have that claim backed up in your résumé. If there is nothing in your work experience, school experience, or other activities that clearly supports the claim, do not put it in. Claims to be "self-directed," "hard-working," "well-organized" and "strong in communication skills" without cross-reference to the résumé quickly doom this résumé to the do-not-interview pile.

EDUCATION HISTORY

Include the following in reverse chronological order:

- Name of university or college
- Address of above
- Program name (include the number of years in the program for college and undergraduate degree programs)
- Dates attended (include graduation dates)
- Standing in class (if it is to your advantage)
- Brief listing of your most relevant courses
- Any educational awards / scholarships received

High school information is not usually included, although if you received some significant honour or award, you may want to include it.

ADDITIONAL TRAINING/COURSES

You may have taken such additional courses as public speaking, writing skills, or auto mechanics. These and hundreds of other courses may have been part of your formal job training or you may have taken courses on your own initiative. Do not overlook these on your résumé. They can serve two very important purposes: first, you have acquired certain skills in these courses; and, second, and equally as important, they show initiative on your part.

EXTRACURRICULAR ACTIVITIES

Include any of your school-related activities, including student government, school newspaper, athletic clubs, and professional associations. If you represented your school at a conference, in an academic competition, or anything else of that nature, get it into the worksheet. As with the courses you took on your own initiative, the skills acquired in those special appointments are not necessarily what is most important; it is the statement the activities make about you. You are multidimensional and someone thought you had some real qualities or you would not have been selected. These and other activities show that you have motivation and can balance a variety of demands upon your time. I cannot think of a career job for a business graduate in which these are not valuable assets.

EMPLOYMENT HISTORY

When you actually start writing your résumé, how you use the information in this worksheet will vary a great deal, depending on what format you select.

The following should appear:

- *Company Name and Address Where You Were Employed*

- *Job Title*

You might have to change it a bit to reflect what you were actually doing.

- *Duties and Responsibilities*

Do not list only your official duties, but include other duties you performed either regularly or occasionally.

- *Accomplishments*

As a graduating student, it is not likely that you can point to how you impacted on the bottom line or increased corporate sales by 17 percent. It is possible, however, that you helped to develop an efficient way of processing orders that came into the warehouse; you were able to deal effectively with customer complaints; you were the top salesperson in the store for three months in a row. Spend time on this section. You may have received some formal recognition for your accomplishment or it may just have been a congratulatory comment from your boss. In the duties section, you have described what you have done. In the accomplishments section, you have shown that you have done it well. It is important to avoid vague generalities when discussing your accomplishments. Claiming you did an excellent job when working in the accounts payable department means little. Quoting, or referring to, a specific comment made by your boss about your performance is much more meaningful.

- *Specific Skills*

These are the special skills you may have learned on the job. Learning how to operate a drill press may not sound particularly important for a business grad, but if you are going to be an industrial cost accountant, this background could be useful. Having used a particular software application may represent the difference between getting an interview or not. Any special skills that demonstrate competence in computer communications and interpersonal skills must be displayed on a résumé.

As you are preparing worksheets, use the above format to include all positions. In most cases, editing will eliminate some of the earlier or less-relevant jobs.

VOLUNTEER EXPERIENCE

A similar format as suggested in the work experience may be used in this section as well. A recurring theme in this worksheet-preparation section has been that it is not necessarily the specific skills you have learned in a particular activity but rather what the experience says about you as a multidimensional person. This is particularly true when it comes to volunteer experience. You have probably picked up some specific skills in your volunteer work that you can list, but equally as important, you are a contributor. This is a quality employers look for in new employees.

OUTSIDE INTERESTS

Aside from work and school, what do you do? What sports or hobbies do you have? These activities may further reinforce your strengths. They might display a well-rounded individual or a specific characteristic such as leadership. This is a worksheet, so feel free to record all your outside interests and activities. Be warned, however, that when you prepare your résumé this section will likely go through some severe editing.

REFERENCES

Although this is an important part of the worksheet preparation process, it is not likely to actually appear on the résumé. This will be discussed later in the chapter. References are, of course, essential. Having a reference from your minister, personal friend, or Member of Parliament is as dated as including height and weight. Previous employers and professors are far better sources.

Before listing any reference, contact that person, get their permission, and try to determine just what they will say about you. I realize that asking that last question is a bit awkward. However, that embarrassment is much less serious than the embarrassment of a weak reference from someone YOU picked. "Damned by faint praise" is a most appropriate quotation. An excellent strategy would be to ask for a letter of recommendation from your previous employer. Depending on your relationship with the person you are contacting, you might even suggest some of the items you would like covered in the letter. If you are still working for an organization, ask for the letter of recommendation before you leave. Some positive comments that you should have in these letters include statements about your performance, specific accomplishments, and the fact that they would hire you again.

Figure 4.1(A). WORKSHEET: YOUR RÉSUMÉ
CAREER OBJECTIVES

What type of job do I want?

What type of organization do I want to work for?

At what level do I want/expect to start?

Figure 4.1(B). WORKSHEET: YOUR RÉSUMÉ
HIGHLIGHTS OF QUALIFICATIONS

The quality and quantity of relevant experience

Education highlights

Educational achievements

Exceptional skill or ability

Figure 4.1(C). WORKSHEET: YOUR RÉSUMÉ
EDUCATION HISTORY

_____

Name of current university or college

_____

Program name and number of years in program

_____

Dates attended, including graduation date

_____

Standing in class

_____

Brief listing of most relevant courses

_____

Educational awards / scholarships received

_____

Figure 4.1(D). WORKSHEET: YOUR RÉSUMÉ
ADDITIONAL TRAINING/COURSES

Job training

Extra courses through school

Additional courses or seminars attended

Figure 4.1(E). WORKSHEET: YOUR RÉSUMÉ
EXTRACURRICULAR ACTIVITIES

_____

Sports activities

_____

School clubs and associations

_____

Professional associations (student chapter)

_____

Other school-related activities

_____

Figure 4.1(F). WORKSHEET: YOUR RÉSUMÉ
EMPLOYMENT HISTORY

Company name and address

Job title

Duties and responsibilities

Accomplishments

Specific skills learned

Figure 4.1(G). WORKSHEET: YOUR RÉSUMÉ
VOLUNTEER EXPERIENCE

Volunteer organization

Title

Responsibilities

Accomplishments

Figure 4.1(H). WORKSHEET: YOUR RÉSUMÉ
OUTSIDE INTERESTS

Sports

Clubs and organizations

Hobbies

Other interests

Figure 4.1(1). WORKSHEET: YOUR RÉSUMÉ
REFERENCES

EMPLOYER REFERENCE #1

Name:

Title:

Company name and address:

Date permission granted:

Reference letter obtained? Yes:____ No: ____

EMPLOYER REFERENCE #2

Name:

Title:

Company name and address:

Date permission granted:

Reference letter obtained? Yes: ____ No: ____

EMPLOYER REFERENCE #3

Name:

Title:

Company name and address:

Date permission granted:

Reference letter obtained? Yes: ____ No: ____

▮▮ The Résumé Format

Finally, you are about to prepare the first draft of your résumé. Take courage, the hard part is done. You completed the necessary research by preparing your worksheets. The first question is, "What format do I use?" Although there is no definite answer to that question, one particular format, the chronological format, may be most suitable for a graduating student.

THE CHRONOLOGICAL FORMAT

A chronological résumé means that you list your more recent job first and work backwards toward your first job (see Figure 4.2). In a sense, every day of your recent life is accounted for. Your start-and-stop dates for each job are displayed, as are the dates you attended various schools. Typically, the most recent and/or the most important jobs get more coverage while earlier, less-relevant jobs get a very pared-down description.

An often-stated disadvantage of this format is that you cannot mask gaps in your life. If this is a problem for you, consider another format. Some books on résumés use as an example a woman who has spent several years away from school or the work force to care for a young family, claiming they can "hide" these years. I have a great deal of difficulty in viewing this as something that needs to be "hidden." Most potential employers would view this candidate very positively. She is mature, has life experience, is ambitious, and has well-developed time-management skills.

The chronological format is best if you are going after your first or second career job with previous work experience confined to part-time, summer, or completely unrelated work. This description fits the majority of graduating students.

Figure 4.2. SAMPLE CHRONOLOGICAL RÉSUMÉ

Paul Johnston
122 Aster Dr.
Charlottetown, Prince Edward Island
C2A 3P9
(902) 555-1237

Career Objective:

Assistant product manager for a manufacturer of packaged goods.

Summary of Qualifications:

Experience in selling to the retail grocery trade
Designed new merchandising tools for employer
Maintained B+ average throughout university
Top student in New Product Development competition
Highly motivated and self-directed
Earned 80 percent of education costs

Education:

University of Prince Edward Island, Charlottetown, Prince
   Edward Island, Bachelor of Business Administration, 1994
Consistently in top 25 percent of class
Awarded Acme Manufacturer Award in New Product
   Development competition

Program Highlights:

Product Management
International Marketing
Marketing Management
Micro Applications for Marketing

Additional Courses:

Oral Communications — Toastmasters
Effective Retail Advertising — Advertising and Sales Club
Lotus for Business, Harvard Graphics, and Ventura —
   Computer Training Institute

Employment History:

Summer of 1992 and 1993:
         Bondar Food Services Ltd.,
         Charlottetown,
         Prince Edward Island
Job Title: Summer Retail Sales Manager

Accomplishments:
> Increased sales level by 12 percent in each of the four territories where I worked
> Developed new merchandising aids for new product introduction

1993 to present:
> White's Building Supply (fall and winter — part time)
> Charlottetown, Prince Edward Island

Job Title: Customer Service Officer

Duties:
> Assist customer in selection of correct products
> Advise customers on proper installation of products
> Supervise newly hired part-time sales staff

Accomplishments:
> Generated additional sales through excellent cross-selling techniques
> Clearly demonstrated correct usage of products
> Twice selected as employee of the month

Additional Employment:

Stocking shelves in supermarket while attending high school
Camp counsellor for two summers

Outside Interests:

Play intramural hockey (cocaptain in 1993)
Member of American Marketing Association (student chapter)
Coach minor hockey
Enjoy cross-country skiing, canoeing and camping

References available upon request.

THE FUNCTIONAL FORMAT

Some students have acquired a lot of relevant experience and corresponding skills. If that is the case for you, the functional format is best. Figure 4.3 presents an example of a functional format. In this format, you display your transferable skills organized under headings. Examples of headings could be: (1) Sales Experience, (2) Technical Expertise, (3) Managerial Experience, (4) Communications Experience. If you are using this format, you would then refer to your worksheets and extract the relevant skills that you gained from your previous jobs or experiences and insert them under the appropriate heading. It is important that skills be clearly categorized along with a brief description. In its purest form, the functional résumé covers up embarrassing gaps as employers and dates are not included.

Figure 4.3. SAMPLE FUNCTIONAL RÉSUMÉ

Angelina Gomez
27 Ocean Blvd.
Pictou, Nova Scotia P2L 4P4
(902) 555-1292

Career Objective:
   To obtain a managerial position in the cost accounting department of a manufacturer.

Experience:
   Technical
   – One year as accounts receivable clerk
   – Six months as cost accounting trainee for a major manufacturer of consumer products
   – One year as cost accountant for a metal fabricator
   Managerial
   – Supervised a staff of five employees in the accounting department
   – Responsible for all training of new employees
   – Prepared biannual employee evaluations
   Communications
   – Prepared detailed monthly reports on manufacturing costs analysis
   – Made major annual presentations to senior executives
   Other Skills
   – Strong computer skills with experience in a broad variety of word processing, accounting, and spreadsheet software

Education:
   Acadia University, Wolfville, Nova Scotia
   Bachelor of Business Administration with Honours

Candidate for graduation, May 1995
Consistently in top third of my class
Have taken additional courses in Leadership, Advanced
Lotus 1–2–3 applications, and Oral Communication

Outside Interests:
Highland dancing, sea kayaking, and travel

References available upon request.

THE COMBINATION RÉSUMÉ

This is a hybrid between the functional and chronological formats. Prepare a functional résumé and then add a separate section showing employers and dates of employment right after the skills section. Figure 4.4 gives you an idea of what the combination résumé looks like.

Figure 4.4. SAMPLE COMBINATION RÉSUMÉ

Camille Bélanger
213 Erable St.
St. Boniface, Manitoba L4B 2R2
(204) 555-9023

Career Objective:
Technical sales representative with manufacturer/distributor of materials and equipment for construction trade.

Summary of Qualifications:
- Candidate for graduation, Bachelor of Management, June 1995
- Completed two years of Civil Technology
- Three years work experience in construction industry
- Maintained "B" average at university
- Elected president of my graduating class
- Excellent and unique combination of technical/business/sales background
- Excellent knowledge of products and equipment used in construction industry

Experience and Skills:
- One year as general labourer on road construction crew
- Two years as heavy equipment operator, including graders, rock crushers, and paving machine
- One year as inside sales person for an industrial supply distributor

Employment History:

1990–91	Johnson Bros. Construction, La Rouge, Saskatchewan
1991–93	Capelli Construction, Winnipeg, Manitoba
1993–94	Marathon Distributors, Winnipeg, Manitoba

Education:
University of Lethbridge, Lethbridge, Alberta,
Bachelor of Management, 1995

Educational Highlights:
- Industrial Selling
- Computer Applications
- Sales Management
- Export Management

Additional Courses:
Quantitative Surveying, Preparing a Sales Proposal

Outside Interests:
Volleyball, fishing, model-ship building, tennis

References available upon request.

■■ Writing the Résumé

With worksheets in hand, you are ready to start writing. Do not worry about layout at this point — get it written first.

USE ACTION VERBS

Your résumé conveys to the reader the skills you can offer. The concise phrasing you use (instead of complete sentences) should start with an action verb that leaves no doubt about the skills or accomplishments that make you a good candidate. The following is a sample list; add your own and do not overuse any one verb.

accomplished	achieved	administered	analyzed
assisted	audited	budgeted	chaired
completed	conducted	controlled	coordinated
counselled	created	delegated	demonstrated
determined	designed	directed	distributed
eliminated	encouraged	ensured	established
estimated	expedited	facilitated	forecasted
formulated	generated	guided	implemented
improved	increased	initiated	innovated
instructed	integrated	interviewed	introduced
launched	lectured	led	liaised
located	lowered	maintained	managed
marketed	merchandised	motivated	negotiated
opened	organized	originated	overhauled
oversaw	participated	performed	persuaded
planned	prepared	presented	programmed
promoted	proved	purchased	recommended
recruited	reduced	reinforced	reorganized
reported	researched	resolved	reviewed
scheduled	selected	sold	streamlined
supported	taught	tested	trained
updated	utilized	witnessed	wrote

PERSONAL DATA

The first section is, of course, your personal data. As mentioned earlier in this chapter, restrict it to your name, address and telephone number. If you are not living at home and it is near the end of term, make sure you arrange to quickly receive, or have forwarded, any mailed responses from potential employers. The same rule applies to the telephone number. As a student, you are rarely at home during business hours. You might want to add another phone number where you know someone will be able to receive your message. A reliable telephone-answering machine might be a good investment. Many machines allow you to access messages from another phone.

JOB OBJECTIVE (OPTIONAL)

Were you able to write a one-sentence statement in the worksheet that accurately described your job objective? Were you able to focus on what you wanted in a career? If you are satisfied with the statement, include it. You are better off with one than without one. Your résumé should be on a disk so you can change the job objective to fit the organization to which you are sending your résumé.

HIGHLIGHTS OF QUALIFICATIONS (OPTIONAL)

The information in your worksheet can be presented in paragraph form:

> Completed degree in Business Administration, achieving the dean's honour list in graduating year. Worked in retail clothing for three years, achieving top salesperson for the month on four occasions. In addition to university courses, have taken courses in public speaking, creative writing, Lotus 1–2–3. Have excellent sales and communication skills.

Perhaps a more effective method of presenting the same information would be in point form using bullets:

- Completed four-year Business Administration degree
- Graduated on dean's honour list
- Three years part-time sales experience in retail clothing
- Top salesperson of the month four times
- Completed additional courses in creative writing and Lotus 1–2–3
- Excellent sales and communication skills

Both formats are acceptable, but the point form with bullets is easier to read. Remember the thirty-seconds rule.

EDUCATION

Prepare this section in reverse chronological order. Assuming you have attended more than one postsecondary institution, give the following information: the degree or diplomas received; the name of the school; the city and province (do not include the school mailing address); and year of graduation.

If graduation is more than six months away, you can state:

> Candidate for graduation, May 1995, Bachelor of Business
>   Management, Ryerson Polytechnic University.
> Major: Accounting
> Class standing: Top 25 percent of class.
> Program highlights: Canadian Income Tax, Managerial Accounting,
>   Financial Management, Micro Applications for Accounting

The class standing or average should be used only if it is to your advantage. Program highlights are optional as well. If you have included them in your "Highlights of Qualifications," it would be redundant to restate them.

If you have had additional courses outside of your school program, list them here in the educational section under the heading "Additional Training/Courses."

EMPLOYMENT HISTORY

Your worksheets have the information. Your challenging task now is to pull out of these worksheets the most important information. By important, I mean those characteristics that sell you. After listing the company name and address, give the job title. Job duties usually come next and, as mentioned earlier, do not just list the official job duties but also some of the other responsibilities that you recorded in your worksheets. You also prepared a section of accomplishments. This section can be integrated with the duties section or included separately. Remember, you have to communicate not just what you did but what you did well. Concise phrasing instead of complete sentences is preferred. Each phrase, ideally, begins with an action verb.

In preparing this section, be careful not to dwell too long on the rather trivial aspects of your job. The various steps in preparing the food in the restaurant are not important, but supervising a shift is. If you have acquired special skills in any of these jobs, include them in the "Accomplishments" section or as an employment subheading titled "Special Skills."

While there are no hard and fast rules for how many jobs you should include in your résumé, two or three is probably plenty. If you have had a number of part-time and summer jobs, detail the two or three most important ones and simply mention the others in one sentence.

In this chapter, I show education coming before employment. This does not have to be the order. The simple criteria is whether you are selling your education or your work experience. If you have had some very relevant work experience, that should go first. If you are seeking your first career job and your work experience is not as relevant, you are selling your education, so put that first.

VOLUNTEER EXPERIENCE (OPTIONAL)

You may have had some volunteer experience that should be high-lighted in your résumé. If the experience is extensive and relevant, you could use a format similar to the one for employment. If your volunteer work does not fit the above criteria, then a brief statement of the type of volunteer work and for whom is sufficient.

OUTSIDE INTERESTS (OPTIONAL)

Be careful! No essays please. I have read some résumés and wondered just when the applicant would find time to work. A brief listing of activities is enough. A blend of passive and active outside interests helps demonstrate your well-rounded character.

REFERENCES

References are essential, but you probably will not include them on your résumé. One school of thought suggests that although an employed candidate does not include references on a résumé, a graduating student can. Most employers, however, do not expect references to appear. A simple statement, "References supplied upon request," is adequate.

▌▌ Packaging the Résumé

Finally! It's written! It's good! Now you have to make it look good. It has to have visual appeal. There are few hard and fast rules other than that the layout must invite one to read it. Several sample layouts are shown on pages 125 to 130. Some print shops have books showing a variety of attractive layouts. Do not make the page(s) look cluttered. If you make the résumé cluttered by trying to get all the information on one page, go to two pages. If two pages are cluttered, you have too much information — probably way too much. Allow very generous borders. Someone devoting thirty seconds to a résumé wants to read down, not across, so a narrow column is preferable. Do not use a variety of fonts. Bold typefaces and indenting can ease the "eye flow" over the page. A good quality bond paper in white, off-white, grey, ivory, or buff is acceptable. Other colours are risky in the conservative business world. The trend in the nineties has been to a more conservative appearance. A good medium-weight bond paper is preferable and you have a variety of choices in texture: linen, pebble, vellum, among others. Whatever paper you pick for your résumé, get additional supplies for your correspondence. Matching envelopes, if available, help with the packaging.

The examples of résumés provided are only a few ways that each job seeker could have presented him- or herself. With all the available variations in format, twenty or more examples would not exhaust the possibilities. There are a variety of publications showing hundreds of good formats, some of which are listed in Appendix B on page 173. I recommend that you go to your library or placement office and peruse these books until you find the format that you prefer.

▮▮ The Covering Letter

Your career planning has allowed you to focus on some general types of careers. Within those categories, a variety of jobs exists, each requiring somewhat different skills. The core skills are probably the same but one job may require more computer skills or more written-communication skills. Perhaps a working knowledge of a particular accounting software package would be useful. Practically speaking, the logistics of preparing a separate résumé for each position for which you are competing is difficult, if not impossible. Having your résumé on disk allows some flexibility, but customizing your résumé to each contact just isn't practical. The answer to this dilemma is a covering letter.

A covering letter has several purposes, but the most important one is to allow the applicant to summarize and focus on those qualifications that should be targeted to the unique requirements of a particular position. It also presents an opportunity to demonstrate one's ability to communicate clearly and effectively. Again, remember that thirty-seconds rule. A well-prepared letter will catch the recruiter's interest and almost compel them to read the résumé. The letter should be concise. Highlight those relevant skills; do not rewrite your résumé.

▌▌ The Covering-Letter Format

Some acceptable variations certainly exist, and the circumstances that caused you to send a résumé will also change the nature of the covering letter. However, the following is a good outline for a covering letter. Figure 4.5 is a sample covering letter that uses the following format:

¶ 1. Introduction and generation of interest
¶ 2. Your value to the company
¶ 3. Background summary
¶ 4. Action to be taken
¶ 5. Statement of appreciation

Each heading is discussed in some detail, and the following is based upon the assumption that the position was not advertised.

PARAGRAPH 1: INTRODUCTION AND GENERATION OF INTEREST

"Derek Viola mentioned that your organization is going through a period of expansion."

"Debra Johnson was telling me you are looking for a sales representative for the Regina Territory. She suggested I contact you."

If I am a recruiter, these opening statements have caught my interest. First of all, you know somebody in my organization (see comments on developing contacts in Chapter 3). You have also shown some knowledge of what is happening to us. You may not always be able to develop a contact, so research on the company is needed. Find out what is going on in the organization, and in the industry. Show that you know something about them. If you obtained your research from recruiting information in your school's placement office, update it. Go through newspapers and publications to find out what has happened recently.

In the next sentence you should introduce yourself. "My name is Scott Dumbrowski and I will be graduating in Honours Business at Wilfrid Laurier University this May."

Avoid the overly sweet complimentary statement. "Your organization is one of the better companies in Canada and has a reputation of being a wonderful place to work." Of course I exaggerate, but be very careful of vague generalizations about how great the company is. If a company has won an award of excellence or done well in some listing of top companies, use that information, by all means.

PARAGRAPH 2: YOUR VALUE TO THE COMPANY

Now you are going to show them what you can do for them. You will be making brief statements about your skills and experience. You want them to be very curious about you. The key for this paragraph is to match your skills and experience to those required by the company. Remember, we are preparing this letter for a company that has not advertised. Again, some research on the company is indicated. If you have, or can develop, a contact among other employees in the company, ask them for information. Get an informational interview. Talk to your professors; they may have had past graduates go through the recruiting process. Phone the human-resources department, or the person for whom you might be working. You will have the added benefit of being able to refer to the conversation in the second paragraph. The better you match your skills to the required skills, the stronger the likelihood that the attached résumé will be read.

PARAGRAPH 3: BACKGROUND SUMMARY

Give a brief synopsis of your relevant education and experience. Again, target those experiences that were most appropriate for this company. You may discover while researching a particular company that they need experience in a particular area that you just happen to have. This did not, however, show up on your résumé. When you were preparing your résumé worksheets, you edited out that experience, believing that others were more important. I am not suggesting that you did a poor job of editing — you had to make choices. Here is an opportunity to highlight the missing experience.

Perhaps you did a school project that included a feasibility study on opening a retirement home. As part of this project, you interviewed seniors to discover their likes and dislikes of existing homes. You also asked which features should be added to retirement homes, and what the monthly rental should be. Your résumé may or may not have mentioned the research project, and even if it was included, perhaps the entry was just a brief comment. You are now sending your résumé to a company that operates a chain of retirement homes. Your covering letter allows you to give a few details about this experience. This point will catch their interest.

PARAGRAPH 4: ACTION TO BE TAKEN

As this covering letter is not in response to an advertisement, you will have to follow up by seizing the initiative. Do not tell them that you hope to hear from them. That is too passive — not a good characteristic for a job hunter. Request an interview, and tell them that you will call to arrange a suitable time. Ideally, this time should be within one to two weeks — sooner than one week and you run the risk of calling before your letter and résumé have been received. After two weeks, your letter and résumé may have been forgotten. Waiting two weeks or more also suggests that following up is not one of your strong points.

PARAGRAPH 5: STATEMENT OF APPRECIATION

Keep it short. "Thank you for your consideration of my application. I look forward to discussing this with you in person."

Figure 4.5. SAMPLE COVERING LETTER

21 Queen Street
Brandon, Manitoba
R1P 0S9

March 1, 1995

Ms. Carmen Dias, Vice-President Sales
Dunham Health Care Products Ltd.
1311 Brock St.
Saskatoon, Saskatchewan S4P 2A3

Dear Ms. Dias:

Derek Viola in your sales department mentioned that your organization is going through a period of expansion in the Canadian market. Recent articles in the business press indicate you are also aggressively seeking out additional international markets. My name is Scott Dumbrowski and I will be graduating in Honours Business at Wilfrid Laurier University this May.

I have had considerable experience in both direct and retail sales and managed to help finance my education through sales commissions. My working knowledge of Spanish and French are other valuable assets for a company seeking international markets. As a member of your sales force, I could manage a sales territory with a minimum of training.

As you can see from my attached résumé, I have maintained a B+ average during my four years at university. Not included on my résumé is a project completed in the systems management course that involved a comparison of the pharmaceutical incompatibility software packages that your retail clients use. Although this was not directly related to your type of operation, it did expose me to the general culture of the industry. My sales experience includes three summers selling house-painting contracts and two years part time selling home entertainment products for Crown Electronics.

I would like the opportunity to discuss employment possibilities with you. I will call by the middle of this month to arrange a time for an interview.

Thank you for your consideration of my application. I look forward to discussing this with you in person.

Sincerely,

Scott Dumbrowski

Encl.

RESPONDING TO ADVERTISED POSITIONS

Although most of the points raised in the previous discussion will not change, there are some rules that you should follow when responding to a job advertisement.

In your opening paragraph, include a reference to the ad, noting the publication, the date that the ad appeared, the file number if one is given, the title of the position, and a brief statement on why you are interested in the job.

Your next two paragraphs follow the format discussed earlier, except that you must target your qualifications, skills, and experience to the stated requirements of the job.

A dilemma that all job seekers face at some point is that they have some of the required qualifications but not all. If these qualifications are something that you clearly do not have, do not apply for the job. You may still send your letter and résumé, pointing out that although you are not qualified for that job, you would be interested in another position. If you have most of the qualifications, do not let the missing ones deter you, particularly if they are not critical. If you are in this position, state your qualifications in paragraph form — the gap will not be so obvious. If you do have all the qualifications, list them in the same order as they appear in the advertisement. You may be one of a hundred responses to this ad. Do some additional research on the company to get a good background, and contact them to see if you can get even more information on what exactly they are looking for. Armed with this extra information, you can be more accurate in targeting your skills and qualifications to the company's requirements — you have given yourself an edge. Of the hundred applicants, eighty know no more about the job than what was in the paper.

The tone of your letter should demonstrate enthusiasm. You are interested and excited about the prospect, and they must know that.

Usually job ads indicate what follow-up action will be taken by the company. If the advertisement is vague, indicate in your letter that you will be contacting them in two weeks to arrange a time for an interview.

THE BROADCAST LETTER

If you have decided to send your résumé out to dozens, or even hundreds, of companies, you still need a covering letter. Before you make the decision to use the broadcast method, be aware that this is not a particularly effective tactic. In a strong economic climate it might uncover a few leads. Otherwise, it can be a colossal waste of time.

There may be some merit in using the broadcast method if you can target a specific industry, indicating that you have unique skills in that area. But still, work all your contacts in that industry first. One student I know has had years of experience in the wilderness-outfitting industry. His job search will include using the contacts built up over the years. There are some manufacturers with which he has had no contact. They are out of province or even out of the country. A broadcast letter accompanied by a résumé may be a useful tactic in these particular circumstances. He can make informed comments on the state of the industry and on his personal objectives. Again, he will contact each recipient of his broadcast letter within two weeks to demonstrate his interest.

▮▮ Conclusion

At the beginning of this chapter you were warned that résumé preparation would be a lot of work. By now you have prepared a number of worksheets, only to edit out most of information you listed. You then prepared several draft résumés, seeking critical evaluations of your work from others. Finally, you had the product you wanted, the layout that invited readership, and the paper stock that provided visual appeal. A lot of work and probably a few dollars have gone into this effort. However, if it's right and does the job, it's a small investment that can help reap big returns.

🗁 Profile: *Susie S. Gray*

- CURRENT POSITION
  Personnel/Payroll Clerk,
  Metro Transportation,
  Municipality of Metro Toronto

- EDUCATION
  Business Administration, Co-op, 1991,
  Seneca College of Applied Arts and Technology

I started working for the Metropolitan Toronto Transportation Department in the contracts section, where I provided technical support related to the Capital Works Program. The ability to keep track of highly detailed responsibilities and tight deadlines was essential to this job. Currently, I am working in the personnel/payroll section, where effective communications and administration are important. With Metro, I have found a wonderful balance between my computer and accounting knowledge. I have come to understand how important formal and informal education are, as well as how invaluable work and volunteer experiences are. Sometimes, regardless of educational preparation, some things seem irrational and political within different organizations. Learning to deal with the logic and compassion of others in any workplace is indispensable.

With the idea of moulding my abilities into solid working knowledge, I enrolled in the Seneca College Business three-year Accounting and Finance Program. After two-and-a-half years in the Accounting and Finance Program, I decided to transfer to the Business Administration Cooperative Program to gain a broader perspective on the business industry.

During my cooperative terms, I worked for two different corporations: the Municipality of Metropolitan Toronto Transportation Department (personnel/payroll section) and the Ontario Municipal Employees Retirement System (OMERS). Before my co-op work experience, I had misconceptions that I would be doing mundane, low-priority jobs that required little or no skills, therefore giving me little opportunity to learn. I was wrong. While working at the Transportation Department, I was exposed to the financial and administrative part of the industry in addition to personnel/payroll duties. Here, I gained much needed experience and insight of personnel and communication skills, knowledge of computer software, and the basic procedure of the payroll system in relation to the work that I now do. With OMERS, I was exposed to the human resources part of the industry. I was involved in recruiting summer students, screening résumés, and interviewing candidates to place the right person with the right skills for the right position.

During my work terms, I became aware of my strengths and turned my weaknesses into positive virtues. I overcame my misconception of the mundane personnel/payroll duties, and learned that no experiences are ever useless — everything has a value and adds up to the sum of my learning experience, knowing myself, and planning a career. One of the most rewarding aspects of these two employment opportunities was in dealing with people. Learning to communicate with my co-workers and other people on a human level played an important role in my everyday life. Through the co-op program, I realized where my future lay.

I participated in varsity sports during my college years at Seneca and was appointed to the Student Athletic Association, becoming vice-president of finance for the committee. I found this a great learning experience for interaction. The responsibility of fund-raising, budget analysis, and interviewing athletes for feedback in order to initiate a more productive system gave me new insight and confidence into other abilities that I have, allowing me to extend myself to bigger challenges.

Upon graduation, I worked for such companies as Eastcom Industries, a small cellular accessories company, doing office administration. After being laid off (a seeming setback, but one that I looked upon as a learning experience), I started using personal contacts and other resources. Soon, I began to work as an administrative assistant in the contract department of Savin Canada, one of the largest photocopier companies in Canada. My accounting knowledge was a valuable asset for the position, and my experience at Savin solidified my background in accounting procedures.

Over the years, I developed a guideline: My future belongs to me in an educational and career-oriented setting. I can take responsibility for my plans and actions, and turn my goals and objectives into reality; I will not allow other people to dictate my career goals. Where do I see myself five to ten years from now? Employed as an administrator within a corporation whose mandate requires progressive thinking and action.

◆

5

THE INTERVIEW

📁 **Profile:** *Michael Van Aelst*

- CURRENT POSITION
  Research Associate
  BBN James Capel Inc.
  Montreal, Quebec
- EDUCATION
  Bachelor of Commerce (with distinction),
  Finance, Marketing (Minor), Concordia
  University, 1992

BBN James Capel is an institutional brokerage firm with a focus on excellence in investment research. The company is owned 50 percent by a Canadian partnership, and 50 percent by James Capel Inc., an international securities house which is one of the oldest stockbroking firms in Britain.

As a research associate, my primary responsibilities include conducting industry analysis and performing detailed ratio analysis of companies' financial statements. I work closely with two investment analysts in trying to determine the appropriate market value of public companies. Industry research requires, among other things, interviewing industry experts and top management of relevant organizations as well as conducting background searches at libraries and government agencies. The investment analysts and I meet with the president, chief financial officer, and other management officials of the companies being analyzed, visit plants, and attend shareholder meetings.

With a Bachelor of Commerce, majoring in Finance, I obtained a solid base of knowledge from which to build upon through direct work experience. Although I knew that I wanted a career in finance, I was uncertain as to the specific career path to pursue. The program at Concordia sparked my interest by introducing me to the investment industry, offering such relevant courses as Investment Analysis. Currently, I am studying to obtain the Chartered Financial Analyst (CFA) designation. This is a very challenging three-year correspondence course, which is virtually becoming a must in the analysis industry.

Although a substantial percentage of jobs appear to be obtained through contacts, I obtained my current position at BBN James Capel through the university career-placement service. There were three significant determinants that helped me to obtain the initial interview with BBN James Capel: my work experience, GPA, and extracurricular activities. During the six months before graduation, and for another nine months after, I was fortunate to have gained some relevant and necessary practical work experience with a retirement planning firm (a position that I also obtained through the university career-placement centre). Throughout my school and university life, I was active in team sports. These helped to build my self-discipline, leadership qualities, and the ability to work in teams and be responsible within a group dynamic.

While searching for employment as a research associate, I took advantage of discussions with friends in the industry, as well as reading up on the available information to determine the skills and characteristics that employers would be searching for. With this knowledge, I was able to market my abilities to match their needs. I also kept myself well informed on economic and political issues and how they affect business. I feel that these preparations were the keys to my success during the interview process at BBN James Capel.

Within the next several years, I hope to obtain the CFA designation and gradually become an investment analyst, a career choice that I expect to pursue over the medium term. The investment analyst is primarily responsible for conducting company analysis, writing reports, presenting ideas to clients and salespeople, and keeping up-to-date with current events. Working for several years in Europe to get a better feel for foreign business practices is a personal interest that I hope will become reality at some point over the next decade. As for my long-range career plans, these remain flexible and will likely change somewhat as I gain more experience and become more aware of the selection of available opportunities.

◆

❙❙ *Introduction*

This is it! You have worked hard to get to this point. A movie actor may practise a scene over and over; the director reshoots a scene dozens of times and then edits together the best bits and pieces to make it look perfect. Unfortunately, you have one shot at an interview and it must be, if not perfect, very good. Nerve wracking? Of course it is! However, as for an actor, preparation is the key. In this chapter we examine the type of preparation needed, interview protocols, typical questions with suggested answers, the employer's objectives in an interview, what not to do, and interview follow-up. Following the procedures in this chapter will not eliminate nervousness. In fact, you do not want to lose your edge, but the suggestions here will make the interview manageable. The key is in being well prepared.

❙❙ Researching the Company

Any interviewer will tell you that one of the easiest ways to "blow" an interview is to know little about that company. As a business student, you are well aware of the various sources of information about companies. It is not enough just to know the number of employees and the products they make. Although that is, of course, essential information, you should also be aware of their competition, where their branch offices are located, the success of any new products, mergers and acquisitions; in fact, anything that is newsworthy about that company.

"I noticed that your organization just landed a contract to supply the ABC Company with components for their lawnmowers. Is this a long-term contract?"

By asking this question, you impressed the interviewer. You obviously picked up this tidbit of information from careful reading of the business press. The answer to the question is of secondary importance; you know that and the interviewer knows that. The fact that you asked the question and had the information is what scored points for you.

Prepare a file for each interview you are going to have. Part of this file will contain both background information and current information on each prospective employer. Larger companies hand out employment or career-path publications and undoubtedly your placement office has them. They typically give background information and the different career paths available in their organization. Of course, you must have that information, but remember, so does every other candidate with whom you are competing. It is current information that can set you apart.

"I noticed your last quarter earnings showed considerable improvement over the previous quarter. To what do you attribute this success?"

You have just stepped ahead of the pack. Aside from the usual secondary sources of information, contacting the company by phone or in person with a well-thought-out set of questions to ask the receptionist can be very productive. Ask lots of questions and ask if some company literature can be sent, or pick it up if you are there in person. Don't worry if the interviewer finds out you have taken these steps — that is a plus.

▋▋ Interview Protocols

GROOMING

Most of us can remember our mother giving us a good last-minute scrubbing while she fussed about our appearance before heading out to a restaurant, church, or visit to an aunt. We probably squirmed and hated the procedure. I have no intention of insulting you by stressing the importance of "packaging the product." You know you have to look your best. Your dress and appearance must also be appropriate. Assuming you are not applying for a position in drama, design, or photography, appropriate dress is usually "business attire."

If you have concerns about what is appropriate, perhaps a friend, placement counsellor, or professor can help guide you. Women project a professional image when they wear a dress (with sleeves) or suit, rather than a blouse and skirt. Simple, classic shoes in a basic colour are best, and pantihose are essential, no matter how hot the weather. For men, a suit is clearly preferable to a sports jacket and slacks. Shirts should be long-sleeved and be either white or in a muted pattern. I love the ties with Mickey Mouse or leaping killer whales, but I surely would not wear one to an interview! Several years ago, a good friend of mine was being interviewed and he noticed the interviewer staring at his shirt. He didn't get the job and when he looked in the mirror he gasped. He had inadvertently put on a T-shirt stamped with "Coors — the breakfast of champions," which was clearly visible under his white shirt. Wear dress shoes — not deck shoes — and matching socks, not white socks.

Perhaps you do not own the appropriate clothes, and funds are typically low as your school years are ending. In the worst financial circumstances, you might consider borrowing clothes. However, an appropriate wardrobe is an investment. Set your interview clothes aside for interviews only. Looking good makes you feel good and feeling good gives you more confidence.

WHAT TO BRING TO THE INTERVIEW

Bring the phone number and the directions to where you are going. Something unavoidable and beyond your control could happen to prevent you from making it on time and although this is indeed unfortunate, phoning the company and letting them know can mitigate the damage.

Paper and pen should be in your attaché case or portfolio case. You may want to have it in front of you when being interviewed. Bring your file on the company; you will probably get an opportunity to review it before being called for the interview. Bring six copies of your résumé with you. You may be interviewed by several people and you can offer to give each a copy. Also, your résumé will make filling out an application form much easier — you will not have to fumble for the dates of past events. Bring letters of reference. You may be asked for them and even if not, you may find an opportune time to offer them.

Bring a list of questions you want to ask your interviewer. These will include questions about the job and about the company. Again, these questions allow you an opportunity to display your knowledge about the company.

School projects. Perhaps you have one or two projects that help demonstrate your skills. Bring an unmarked version of the project and put it in your case. A business student, unlike a design student, does not generally carry a portfolio of work. However, there may be an opportunity to show it. A word of caution: do not force this project on an interviewer. If it is a rather lengthy paper, they have neither the time nor the inclination to read it. Perhaps you might leave it with them. This would then serve as a good reason for additional follow-up. If you prepared executive summaries of your report, it may be more appropriate to offer these.

WHEN TO ARRIVE

Do not be late. If you are unfamiliar with the location, a dry run the day before could be helpful. If distance makes this impractical, leave enough time to get to the location well before the time of the interview. The flat tire, traffic congestion, or bad weather can be handled with less stress if you know you have plenty of time. If you arrive in the area forty minutes early, don't go in. Arriving five to ten minutes early is better. If you are too early, they will not be ready for you and you appear to be overanxious.

THE MOMENT BEFORE THE INTERVIEW

Typically, you have a few minutes to wait before being called in. You may also be at the height of your nervousness. Take a few deep breaths. Review your file on the company and the list of questions you want to ask. Remind yourself that you really are ready for this interview. They selected you from a long list of applicants and only a handful of short-listed candidates made it this far. You know yourself and your strengths; your personal inventory-taking brought that into focus. You have a great résumé and you have researched the company. You have prepared yourself for some tough questions and you know the type of answers you want to give. (A detailed discussion on types of questions will be found later in this chapter.) You can be confident, not cocky, just confident.

WALKING INTO THE INTERVIEW ROOM

So much happens in ten seconds. The interviewers have a good look at you. They watch your body language, how you respond to their greeting, your level of anxiety, your handshake, your smile, your eye contact. What happens in this ten seconds is very important. A limp handshake or poor eye contact has put you into a hole that is hard to get out of. On a more positive note, if first impressions are positive, you have already gained an advantage. Walk into the room with confidence, make eye contact with everybody, give the interviewer an opportunity to offer their handshake first and follow instructions, which will likely be, "Take a chair." When the interviewers introduce themselves, it's a good idea to repeat their names. "Pleased to meet you, Ms. Chan." This is particularly useful in helping you to remember names when there are several people involved.

■■ "Let the Play Begin"

You're on now. All the work you have done is about to pay off. Unlike a play, however, you do not have a script. Only the interviewer has one. Interviewers are a varied lot. The questions they ask, the way they ask, the way they respond to your answers, and what particular qualities in a candidate they are looking for differ, sometimes significantly. However, certain questions, or at least categories of questions, are commonly asked. Some are difficult and others are quite straightforward. Most interviewers are skilled but some are not. Some want you to feel comfortable, believing that they can find out more about a person who is relaxed, while a few conduct stress interviews to see how you react under pressure. If you take enough interviews, you will have a variety of experiences.

In this section, some of the more commonly asked questions are presented, along with suggestions on how to answer them. Obviously, these can only be suggestions. A "canned" response will not impress an interviewer. A carefully thought out response that was prepared because you anticipated the particular question, will.

There is no point in trying to rehearse answers. Just think about the ways that certain questions could be handled; not a memorization, but, rather, the information that you would like to give to the interviewer. Reread the self-assessment you completed at the beginning of your career-planning process. If you did that job well, and it is fresh in your mind, you have the information needed to respond to most of the questions that will come up. You have probably had to present reports to your class, a group that tends to revel in throwing out hard questions. If you worked hard on your project and had it well prepared, you probably handled those tough questions well. The interview you are about to attend will not likely be very different. A thorough self-assessment will provide you with that same self-confidence.

Listing even a fraction of the questions that might be asked would be impossible. On the next few pages a sampling of some of the most often asked questions is presented.

- *Tell me about yourself.*

This is a common request — prepare for it. It is not an invitation to tell your life story. It is an opportunity to focus on the strengths you listed on your personal inventory worksheets. Ask the interviewer if he/she wants you to focus on your personal life, your academic life, or your working life. It might be one or all three of the above.

- *When you were at school, what extracurricular activities did you participate in?*

Participation in extracurricular activities shows initiative and suggests that you are a well-balanced individual. Be prepared to comment briefly on some aspect of your activities. If you did not participate in any, perhaps it was because you had a demanding part-time job or you had parenting responsibilities. Don't just say you did not participate — indicate why.

- *At school, what subjects did you like the most and the least? Why?*

The emphasis is on what you liked the most. Try to tie in how the ones you liked the most work with the skills required for this job. Be careful when discussing the ones you liked the least. You might comment that you did not like the marketing courses as much as the other courses, but you realize the importance of learning about marketing. We assume you are not being interviewed for a marketing position.

- *How did you finance your education?*

The larger the proportion of your education that you paid for, the better. Interviewers know how tough it is to be completely self-support-ing while attending school. They do want to hear, however, that you contributed to the costs by working summers and/or part-time while attending school. Many, if not most, students have used a student loan/grant from a provincial government. This is quite normal and not something to hide from the interviewer.

- *What do you think about your professors?*

Careful! You may well have had a mixture of good and not so good ones. This is no time to vent your spleen about how bad a particular professor was. You can hedge by commenting that while they differed in approach you believe they provided you with a solid background.

- *Why did you pick this school?*

Not because it was closest to home. Give a more positive response. You picked it because after careful research, you concluded that it offered one of the best programs available.

- *Why did you pick a college instead of a university?*

Those of you in college will get this question. The employers are not putting down college; they just want to see how you can handle this stressful question. You can emphasize the practical versus theoretical approach and how the courses offered fit in with what you wanted. Tell them how your research into schools revealed the strong reputation of the program/college in which you enrolled.

- *Did you work as hard as you could have done at school?*

You probably did work hard but you could have worked harder. Depending on your circumstances, you can briefly discuss other events in your life, such as part-time jobs, extracurricular activities, or family responsibilities that took away from time spent on school work. Employers would rather have a well-rounded person or a person who had to sacrifice to be able to afford to attend school than one who did nothing but work on their courses.

- *What was your standing in the class?*

Many of the comments in the previous question could be adapted here. If your standing was not particularly high, there is also a way of expressing your standing. If you stand twentieth in a class of forty-two students, you were in the top half. If you were a bit below that point you were "about midpoint in the class."

- *Why do you want to work for us?*

Your research will now pay off. You can make comments about changes in the company, reputation, recent performance, and how you find the direction the company is taking to be exciting. You want to be part of this exciting future. This question is very likely to be asked.

- *What kind of skills do you bring to this job?*

Another opportunity to sell yourself. Earlier we mentioned the trend toward "bottom-line" hiring. What can you do for me today? State the transferable skills you have developed. An ability to communicate, certain computer skills, and a skill in managerial accounting are some of the transferable skills you listed in your personal inventory.

- *Are you willing to relocate?*

Some organizations do not want a person who is determined to stay in their home area. Obviously, an unwillingness to relocate cuts down on your options. If you really don't want to move, you might just as well be honest about it. How far away, the circumstances surrounding a relocation, and the frequency of moving may be factors in your decision. If that is the case, answer "yes." Without that answer, you might not have the option of accepting or rejecting an offer.

- *What did you dislike about your last job?*

If your job experience has been summer jobs and part-time jobs only, you have performed some pretty mundane tasks. Couch your response in both positive and negative terms. You did not care for the lack of challenge in certain aspects of the jobs but you were still able to learn and gain worthwhile experience from every one of them. A point to remember. You must answer the question being asked but you can frame your responses in a positive way. The next question illustrates this.

- *What were the bad characteristics of your last boss?*

As with the earlier question about your professors, your last boss did not have many, or any, bad characteristics. He might, however, have been so busy you didn't have much of an opportunity to seek guidance from him. Another boss was not hard-nosed and arrogant but, instead, was rather demanding, which allowed you to learn a great deal. If you give a lot of negative answers about school, professors, jobs, and bosses, even when you are encouraged to do so, you are being led down the garden path.

- *If you start work with us, how long would you expect to stay?*

The interviewer is now smiling inwardly. "Let's see how she handles that one!" Obviously, do not give a specific time-frame. Let them know you are looking for a career position where you can hope to grow professionally and be able to assume more responsibilities as you gain experience, and you also believe that their organization offers those opportunities. You are really telling them that you do not view this company as a stepping stone to something better or that you will stagnate and spend the rest of your life in a routine, boring position.

- *Where do you expect to be five years from now?*

Another very common question. It doesn't hurt to turn the tables and ask what opportunities the company offers to someone who works hard, is anxious to learn and develop, and is capable. Their answer probably describes just where you want to be in five years.

- *Why should I hire you?*

Marry your strengths to their needs. It's that simple. You know your strengths and, either through prior research or through the conversation during the interview, you have a good idea what their needs are. In fact, you may have had an opportunity earlier to ask them what they are looking for in a candidate. Tie into those needs whenever possible.

- *What interests you about this job?*

This is related to the previous questions; it's just coming from the opposite direction. Again, your research on the company will pay off. You could also ask the interviewer for more details about the position, again allowing you to make that all-important match of their needs with your skills.

- *Do you prefer working alone or with others?*

Do not treat this as an either/or question. Any knowledge you have about the job will help in answering the question, but you do not want to give the impression that you are hard to get along with or that you have little initiative and creativity. Indicating that you like a blend of both may be an appropriate response depending upon circumstances.

- *Are you a leader or a follower? Illustrate your answer with examples.*

Most of us truly have a blend of both characteristics. Show them that. You may slant your response a bit toward the leadership side of the equation. Remember, there are many forms of leadership. Some people are quietly effective in leading others. You might refer to some group project you did at school in which you had to encourage other workers to get involved. On another project, you learned from other students when they took a leadership role. The interviewer will also want to know if you can follow instructions.

- *Give me an example in which you had to deal with a difficult challenge and tell me how you met that challenge.*

Step one is to outline the challenge. As a student, perhaps the most difficult (and common) challenge is balancing all the demands on your time. Pick one event that particularly stands out. Perhaps several assignments were due at once, your employer at your part-time job wanted you to work more hours, and your hockey team was in the playoffs. Demonstrate how you organized your time and managed the situation — successfully, of course.

- *What is your greatest weakness?*

What an opportunity to talk yourself out of a job. Believe it — the interviewer has that same inward smile again. Any weakness you wish to mention will not be so much a weakness as perhaps inexperience in a relatively unimportant aspect of the job. At the same time, stress your ability to learn quickly and gain experience.

- *How do you handle rejection?*

If the interviewer represents a manufacturer of food products and you are looking for a sales position, you had better make it clear that you handle rejection well. Let them know that rejection is not taken personally and that it is quite normal to have several rejections before you gain acceptance. Above all, show that rejection does not make you feel defeated, but rather determined.

- *What kind of people do you not like to work with?*

This is not a trick question. You probably do not like to work with people who are chronic complainers, who are slack, or who do not care about their work. By stating this, you are letting the interviewer know what you are not like that.

- *Give me an example that shows your initiative.*

Your best examples probably come from your work experience or school experience. Perhaps you sorted out a better way of doing something at work or you took on responsibility not expected of you. Perhaps you organized a club or a sports team. What you did may not be as important as the fact that you showed initiative.

FINAL QUESTIONS

Toward the end of the interview you may be asked if you have any questions, and of course you do. If you have not already discussed the particulars about the job, ask about them now. Ask if there will be any additional interviews. If no, ask when decisions will be made. Do not push it — just let them know you are very keen on the job. If additional interviews will be held, ask if it is possible to schedule the next one. They probably will not, but you will lose nothing by trying. If you are offered the job, be enthusiastic. You do not have to accept it on the spot. They may indicate when they want to hear from you or ask when you will be able to make your decision. Even if you have doubts, show this enthusiasm. You can turn it down when you have an opportunity to weigh the pros and cons, or better yet, compare it to other offers.

On exiting, leave as you entered, a firm handshake while thanking them by name and a good closing statement, repeating how enthused you are about the exciting prospect you have been discussing. If it has not already been determined, find out when you will be speaking again.

📁 Profile: *Jamie O'Neil*

- CURRENT POSITION

  Senior Accountant
  KPMG Peat Marwick Thorne
  Dartmouth, Nova Scotia

- EDUCATION

  Bachelor of Commerce, Accounting (Magna Cum Laude), 1992, Saint Mary's University

As a senior accountant at KPMG Peat Marwick Thorne, I am gaining practical experience in auditing, accounting, and tax by performing audits of various organizations. Auditing involves an examination of the accounting records of an organization and testing the information for the purpose of issuing a set of financial statements and an opinion whether the statements are materially correct. With the exception of not-for-profit organizations, such engagements also encompass the preparation of tax returns, both individual and corporate. Working in such a service-oriented organization requires that one be able to build a rapport with clients, recognize their needs, and deliver a quality product. As such, the accounting profession involves marketing oneself, the firm, and the various services available to both existing and potential clients. The hands-on experience is combined with a number of courses and examinations that will eventually earn me the designation of Chartered Accountant (CA).

My career path began while at Saint Mary's University with my decision to major in Accounting. I enrolled in courses that provided the necessary exemptions once in the CA program. But I also took courses that were of particular interest to me, or that would provide me with knowledge or experience outside of the accounting and commerce areas. Two of the courses I found to be particularly valuable were International Management and Entrepreneurship. The first involved researching the management techniques and environment, business and otherwise, of a foreign country and presenting one's research to others in the course. The latter involved taking a product or idea and creating a viable business plan for presentation to a simulated board of financiers. Each course required a great deal of independence and commitment — each emphasized learning through experience rather than through teaching. Presenting the results of my research to my peers was a valuable experience that enabled me to improve my public speaking skills.

Saint Mary's also provided a wide variety of extracurricular activities that included various societies and clubs on campus, as well as Career Days and the annual Business Dinner. These activities provided me with the opportunity to meet new people and become involved in the university. As an alumnus of Saint Mary's, I remain involved, by helping to organize various alumni events and through my support of varsity athletics.

Prior to working with KPMG Peat Marwick Thorne, I held a summer job as a contracts-accounting assistant with LASMO Nova Scotia Limited, a company in a joint venture with the Province of Nova Scotia in Canada's first offshore oil development. This job eventually led to part-time work during the months I was enrolled in university. I was given the responsibility of reviewing, auditing, and correcting contractor invoices on an $18 million reimbursable contract to ensure payment within its terms. In addition, I collected various costing information and presented it on a spreadsheet to keep various individuals abreast of commitments and expenditures. My experience at LASMO was valuable because I learned to handle responsibility and how to manage my time appropriately between my job and university.

In the fall of my graduating year, I applied to various accounting firms. I researched each of the firms to which I had applied by reading their recruiting brochures and by considering the attributes they were seeking in potential employees and how I had demonstrated such qualities in my past work history, community involvement, and in university. In the interviews I was able to ask intelligent questions about each of the firms. I worked on building a rapport with the people with whom I came into contact and marketing myself to them because I realized that those were important qualities that they would be seeking in a staff accountant. I evaluated each of the firms by considering my first impressions and their philosophies. In the end, my decision to accept a position with KPMG was an easy one because it came down to feeling comfortable with the people with whom I would be working.

I am currently finishing my second year with KPMG Peat Marwick

Thorne and am preparing to write the Uniform Final Exam — the final hurdle in obtaining my CA designation, which will provide me with new challenges and opportunities to work abroad, to become a specialist in a particular area (i.e., tax, environmental auditing), or to make the move to private industry.

◆

❚❚ The Employer's Objectives

As a business student, you are aware of the importance of knowing a customer's needs. It is no different in an interview; you are selling something — yourself. Each position has somewhat different needs. Your earlier research and carefully crafted questions will allow you to gain an insight into those specific needs. There are, however, a number of generic skills that interviewers tend to look for. Rarely will they ask outright if you possess these skills or characteristics, but rather will determine this information from how you respond to a series of seemingly unrelated questions. Other interviewers may be more direct and ask you just what you have done that demonstrates this skill or characteristic.

In the following section we examine these most sought-after skills and characteristics and the questions an employer might use to determine your strengths and weaknesses in these areas.

COMMUNICATION

This is one of the most sought-after skills and one that is not too difficult to assess. Any open-ended question requiring your answer in paragraphs — not short answers — displays your communication skills. Examples of questions that allow the interviewer to assess your communication skills are listed below.

- *Tell me about yourself.*
- *Tell me about the jobs you have had and what you liked and disliked about each one.*
- *Tell me about your school.*

LEADERSHIP

In most positions, leadership is important. If you are being interviewed for a managerial position or a position that logically leads to management, you will need to show leadership. What are your personal strengths and what have you done that demonstrates those strengths? It is up to you to display "leadership." This can be demonstrated by your having served on the executive of some club or organization, having been a captain of a sports club, coached in some sport, or simply been the one who tends to lead in group projects.

ABILITY TO WORK WITH OTHERS

Despite the nature of the job for which you might be applying, you will have to work with others.

- *Do you prefer working alone or in a team?*
- *What problems have you run into when working with others in your previous jobs? What about at school?*

AMBITION

- *Where do you hope to be in five years? (almost a standard question)*
- *What are the characteristics that allow one person to succeed while another does not?*

ORGANIZATIONAL SKILLS

- *You have five courses, all with assignments due within a month, two term tests and a part-time job. What strategies would you use to cope?*

INITIATIVE

- *Give me an example that demonstrates your initiative.*
- *What have you done that sets you apart from the average student?*

RESPONSIBILITY

- *What type of supervision do you prefer?*
- *What kind of challenge are you looking for in your next job?*

FLEXIBILITY

- *Tell me about a major change in your life. How did you deal with it?*

- *When did you select your major field of study? Prior to that, what did you want to study and why did you change?*

ENERGY LEVEL

- *Describe a typical week in your life.*

Enthusiasm, friendliness, assertiveness, and self-confidence are other qualities the interviewer will be looking for. These characteristics may be displayed by specific answers to specific questions or by your general demeanour.

INTERVIEWER'S RATING SHEET

Although the use of a scaled rating sheet is far from universal, it is not uncommon. Even those interviewers who do not have a formal rating sheet are likely to be doing much the same thing on a mental level throughout the interview. Figure 5.1 is a typical rating sheet.

Figure 5.1. TYPICAL INTERVIEW RATING SHEET

Appearance

1	2	3	4	5
Poorly groomed				Well-groomed with appropriate dress

Knowledge of Company

1	2	3	4	5
Knows nothing about company				Great deal of knowledge about company, including recent developments

Knowledge of Job

1	2	3	4	5
Knows nothing of job				Thoroughly researched the job

Experience

1	2	3	4	5
No related experience				Considerable related experience

Communication Skills

1	2	3	4	5
Very poor communication				Outstanding communication skills

Self-Confidence/Poise

1	2	3	4	5
Very nervous, lack of any self-confidence				Remarkable poise, very confident

Enthusiasm

1	2	3	4	5
Very dull, no enthusiasm				Very enthusiastic and interesting

Intelligence

1	2	3	4	5
Did not understand questions, confused				Very quick and alert, readily understood complex questions

Social Skills

1	2	3	4	5
Cold, unfriendly				Friendly, warm personality

Interest in Job

1	2	3	4	5
Not interested				Keenly interested in job and company

Career Goals

1	2	3	4	5
Has no idea what he/she is looking for in career				Has very clear and realistic career goals

▮▮ Interview Follow-Up

THE FOLLOW-UP LETTER

A follow-up to each interview is a must! It is surprising how many candidates miss this absolutely essential step. Write a thank-you letter the same day you had the interview while events are still fresh in your mind. The letter can help put your name on the "interview again" file, or viewed more negatively, help to ensure you do not end up on the "do-not-short-list" file.

In this letter, you will be accomplishing several things. First, do the courtesy of thanking them for their time and giving you an opportunity to discuss employment possibilities. You can also restate your enthusiasm for the job for which you were interviewed, and some specific aspects about the company that impressed you. If you had the perfect interview, a rare occurrence indeed, than you can reinforce the comments made in the interview that tied your skills to the job requirements. Figure 5.2 is a sample follow-up letter.

Figure 5.2. SAMPLE FOLLOW-UP LETTER

March 17, 1994

Ms. Joan Gaulin
Manager, Human Resources
Ralsten Packing Ltd.
23 Edward St.
Hull, Quebec

Dear Ms. Gaulin,

Thank you for the opportunity to discuss the employment opportunity in your cost accounting department. I enjoyed meeting you and learning more about the fairly complex nature of your business. The emerging international opportunities for Ralston Packing sound very exciting.

The expansion plans for your organization, both in the domestic and international market, stimulate my interest as international business travel particularly appeals to me. My working knowledge of English, French, and German would be an asset in this environment. My high academic standing in the accounting courses do indicate an ability to learn quickly. New challenges presented by your recent acquisition of Traders Enterprises offer an exciting future — a future I would like to share.

Again, thank you for considering my candidacy. I look forward to hearing from you next week.

Sincerely,

Chantal Joannisse

Typically, you will leave the interview realizing that you did not communicate to the interviewer some of your important strengths. Your letter is an opportunity to let them know what they are. Remember, however, this is not an essay, just a one-page letter. If specific action was discussed regarding when you might hear from them or when you might contact them, reiterate it.

If you were interviewed by more than one person, send each interviewer a letter. Confirm the spelling of the name and the title of each individual. Again, send the letter out *immediately* after the interview. Sending it by fax is preferable.

THE INTERVIEW FILE

The other post-interview task is entering data on your interview file. This file already should contain your research on the company, the name and address of the organization, contact person(s) (update file with any additional people you may have met), date of interview, nature of job, likes and dislikes of position, interview improvements needed, and date and method of follow-up. Keep this file current.

THE PERSONAL FOLLOW-UP

Never let the job opportunity drift off into the sunset. Perhaps you have a time-frame for further contact that was established at the end of the interview. If they said they would contact you in a week's time, allow one extra day and then contact them. Do not point out that they were late in getting to you; just stress again that you are very interested in the job and want to know where things stand at the moment. If the contact says that no decision has been made, you might say, "If it's all right with you, I'll contact you again next week." You could further ask, "Is there anything I can do in the meantime to help convince your organization that I am the right person for the job?" Aggressive? Yes! A good approach? Absolutely! If you get a rejection you have very little to lose. Why not ask for another opportunity to convince him or her that you really are the best person for the job? If that fails, ask if there are other opportunities within the organization and if you could have the name of someone else that might be interested in talking to you. Being persistent and aggressive are positives, not negatives. Nobody wants a candidate that gives up easily.

▪▪ Subsequent Interviews

There is nothing standard about the number of interviews a company puts its candidates through. Typically, in the subsequent interviews you will meet other people in the organization. If your first interview was with someone from the human resources department, the next one will likely involve your potential supervisor. Many of the things you had to accomplish in the first interview will have to be redone. As well, you may be called on to demonstrate how much you know about the company and more details on what skills you have to offer.

You may also be confronted with aptitude tests and personality tests. Do not let these add to your anxiety — they are designed to ensure the employer gets the right "fit" for the company. They are in your best interests as well. You should also be armed with additional questions about the job. They should be less general than the questions you asked in the first interview. As a matter of fact, you have been able to refine and add questions based on what you found out in the interview.

One big question that students approach with trepidation is salaries. DO NOT ask about salary, holidays, or benefits in the first interview. In a subsequent interview, there is a strong possibility the issue will be raised by the employer. If not, and you are asked if you have any questions, it is acceptable to ask about the salary range. Do not ask about benefits and holidays. That can be discussed when an offer is made. If you are asked what your salary expectations are, you have a bit of a challenge. Know in advance what the salary range is for that industry or for graduates in your program. Your placement office has those statistics. If you were able to determine that the average starting salary was, say, $26,000 per annum, and your background is fairly typical of all graduates in your class, then respond by giving the range, not an exact amount. I suggest using the average salary as the bottom figure in the range and respond by saying, "Between $26,000 and $30,000." You know you are worth at least the average. Do not undersell yourself; after all, you may well be entering into negotiations. I am not suggesting that you should reject an offer simply because it is lower than the average of your class. There are so many other and more important factors to consider.

This chapter on interviewing opened with an emphasis on the importance of preparation before an interview. In a sense, this was misleading. Your preparation will not end until you have secured your job. It is most likely you will have several rejections before an acceptance. It is tough to avoid getting down after being rejected. However, rise above it and use the experience to prepare yourself better for the next interview. Just as a stage actor becomes better with practice, so will you.

▌▌ Conclusion

As I write the final chapter of this book, I think of one of my students who is a few months away from graduation. She is a woman who returned to school after fourteen years of working and raising a family. She is about to have her second interview with a manufacturer of high-tech medical equipment that is used primarily for senior citizens. The company has experienced strong growth, particularly in international markets, which represent 70 percent of their total sales. As a business student, you will instantly recognize that this is a company well positioned to enter the next century — it uses and develops leading-edge technology. The ultimate client base is senior citizens, a growing segment of our society. This company has an international perspective so necessary in an emerging global economy. As this book stated, part of career planning involves identifying those companies that should experience growth even in a flat or sluggish economy.

In this particular situation, the company had advertised for an "administrative assistant" to the director of marketing. Not surprisingly, over 200 responses were received. As you read this, the numbers may seem daunting. After all, how could you as a fresh graduate ever survive such odds? Let us examine what the student did to improve the odds. Some months ago, she had thoroughly prepared her self-assessment, and was able to identify her strengths and transferable skills. She had discovered, in this process, what she wanted and did not want in a job. She wanted challenge and the opportunity to be self-directed on the job. She determined that travel was not a problem but relocation was. In short, she knew herself. She had been developing her network and had several good contacts in the business world, particularly in her community. Self-assessment led to a well-prepared résumé that went through several drafts before she was satisfied.

When the advertisement appeared, she was ready. She had a personal contact, not in the company, but one that knew someone who was. Through that source, and by scanning newspapers and business publication files, she gathered a lot of recent and relevant information. The covering letter that accompanied her résumé mentioned the contact's name and made several references to the information on the company that she had gathered. She hand-delivered the package to the company, and a few days later followed up with a phone call to see what progress had been made. She was told that she was one of ten selected for an interview.

By the time the interview was to take place, she had reviewed all the information on the company, the self-assessment and the inventory of transferable skills, and she was ready. She was experiencing a blend of apprehension and confidence, the confidence coming from her high level of preparedness that started months ago.

In the course of the interview her preparation allowed her to answer all the questions without being "thrown." By the time she had answered a series of questions probing her knowledge of the company, the interviewer joked, "You know more about the company than I do!" She was asked detailed questions about her courses at school. The interviewer was particularly interested in some of her projects. Our student had brought several with her and the two of them spent considerable time going over them. This is far from typical, but it happened and she was ready.

After the interview the student sent a follow-up letter thanking the interviewer and mentioning how keen she was on the prospect of working for that company. A few of the issues raised in the interview were also included. Twenty-four hours later she got a phone call informing her that she was now on a short list of five candidates. Having had the presence of mind to ask who she might be meeting at this second interview, she will be well prepared. Remember, this competition started with over two hundred, and now there are five. At the time of writing, she has not yet had the second interview.

Although our candidate will unquestionably make an excellent employee if hired, so would some of the 200 or so rejected applicants. Why did they not make the grade? It was not lack of experience. It was not lack of transferable skills, nor lack of enthusiasm. They did not know the process involved in career planning. Some of their own skills or strengths were not recognized, which meant they did not know clearly the type of career that could best utilize those skills. Their résumés could not possibly show them to advantage if they themselves did not know what their strengths were. They may not have thought to research the company, develop contacts, or even include a covering letter. They had no chance against those who did know the process, and how to shorten very long odds.

You have something valuable to offer the business world — you are not one of the two hundred or two thousand. Your unique strengths are there. Uncover them and use the strategies I have outlined. With hard work, you will be one of one.

📁 Profile: *Shelly Repka*

- CURRENT POSITION

  Marketing Coordinator
  Rogers Cantel Inc.
  Calgary, Alberta

- EDUCATION

  Co-op Business Administration Diploma,
  Marketing, 1990, Southern Alberta Institute
  of Technology

I am the marketing coordinator for southern Alberta at Rogers Cantel Inc. I work in a dynamic environment in the Calgary office with the Alberta team, which consists of various departments — Sales, Marketing, Customer Service, Engineering, and Network Operations. As the marketing coordinator, I work closely with the sales department. I assist the sales team with support at various events and promotions. The objective of the promotions is to obtain leads and create sales. For example, I work with the dealer sales manager and as a team, we present sales incentives and customer promotions to the distributors. I also assist the major account executive in planning and organizing events to entertain or train the major accounts.

My education at Southern Alberta Institute of Technology (SAIT) helped me to develop verbal and written communication skills, computer skills, and organizational skills. In addition, as a co-op Marketing student I worked with the Tourism Industry of Alberta and the Alberta Lung Association during my work terms. The work terms were not just another job, but a work experience that gave me first-hand marketing knowledge about industries in which I was interested.

I also networked in the business community in Calgary. I researched certain industries and companies to learn more about opportunities. I wanted to be involved in an industry that was relatively new and growing. I chose telecommunications since there are many opportunities and challenges.

After graduating from SAIT in December of 1990, I worked on various contracts to gain direct marketing experience. In addition, I wanted an insight into the different opportunities in the marketing field.

In April of 1991, Cantel was looking to hire two people for a four-month contract to assist with special events and sponsorships during the summer. Cantel wanted a current co-op student and a graduate from the co-op Marketing program. My résumé was on file at the SAIT Student Employment Centre and was forwarded to the Cantel office. I went through two interview sessions and was then offered the four-month contract. Even though I had wanted a full-time job, I took the contract.

I welcomed the opportunity to experience the world of telecommunications at an entry-level position as a "Roving Phone Booth." After the four months, the contract was extended and then a full-time position became available. Cantel needed a full-time marketing coordinator for Southern Alberta. I submitted my application, along with many other people across Canada, and once again went through various interview sessions and was then chosen for the job.

This experience made me realize many things about searching for a job. First of all, do your "homework." Research the company by visiting the local library and reading a copy of the annual report. Call Customer Service, and ask questions, talk to customers, the receptionist, or suppliers. During the interview, be positive and ask questions. Also, if you really want the job, ask for it!

Once you accept a position, show an interest in learning as much as you can about the company and other departments, especially if you are hired on a contract basis. This gives you an excellent opportunity to see if there is a "fit" for both of you (the employer and the employee).

My ten-year goal is to become a marketing director in the telecommunications industry with responsibilities in planning, organizing, motivating, and controlling the region's marketing efforts. To help ensure that I attain my goal, I plan to acquire a Commerce degree, majoring in marketing. In addition, I plan each business quarter with objectives to keep me "on track." I believe education, perseverance, and determination are going to assist me in reaching my goals.

◆

Appendix A: Hi-Tech Tips for
              Your Job Search

■■ The Computer Disk, Your Résumé and Covering Letter

To create your résumé and covering letter, you have a few choices. You can hire a print shop to typeset your résumé, which is fairly inexpensive, but there are drawbacks. The multiple copies of the résumés are inexpensive per unit, but the single, job-specific, covering letter can be very expensive. The covering letter and the résumé should be of the same paper stock and typeface, so having a print shop create your résumés may not be the most practical option. Using a personal computer is a better solution for most people.

On a computer you can create your résumés on demand; you are not forced to make a large number of copies to save money at a print shop. You can easily update your résumé, and you can create somewhat different versions of it for specific companies. The computer also allows you to customize each covering letter. The type of printer is important. A dot-matrix printer, although inexpensive and reliable, does not have a print quality that is acceptable in today's business environment. An ink-jet type of printer is an inexpensive option that produces high-quality outputs. Of course, a laser printer offers the highest quality, but the cost can be prohibitive.

■■ Mail Merge and the Covering Letter

Most word-processing packages have a mail-merge feature. If you have developed a mailing list of companies to whom you wish to send a résumé/covering-letter package, the mail merge can be a real time-saver. Just merge each name and address with a copy of your covering letter. Although the text of the covering letter will vary somewhat with the circumstances, much, perhaps most, of the text will be constant. Create a letter that uses your mailing-list information and leave blank sections to customize your letter. You should also create, if your printer allows it, a merge file for envelopes. Having a printed envelope makes your package look that much better. A note of caution! Never let your quest for efficiency hurt the personalized aspect of your covering letter.

▌▌ Résumé Software Packages

Several résumé kits or software packages are on the market. Basically you load the data from the worksheets you have prepared into the program. The program then organizes the data, and with some instructions from you, out comes a résumé. Although this description is highly simplified, that is the basic purpose. My concern is that these packages may take away your own creativity and produce a good, average résumé. If you think back to the thirty-seconds rule — the amount of time a recruiter looks at a résumé — average is not good enough. Your résumé has to stand out from all the others.

This criticism may not be entirely fair. New software packages are coming out, and some may do an excellent job. Review these, if possible. They might become better.

▌▌ Scheduling Your Job-Search Activities

There are some excellent scheduler software packages on the market. They can be a real boon to your time management. Different program bundles have schedulers built into them, or, if you do not have one of these, specific packages are not expensive. Your electronic calendar may tell you on a particular day that you need to make five new contacts, send out three résumés, which companies need a call that day to confirm that they received your résumé, what post-interview call-backs you will be making, and so on. Properly set up, the software package will allow you to manage more contacts at one time without letting things "slip through the crack."

Appendix B: Suggested Readings

Beatty, Richard H. *175 High-Impact Cover Letters*. New York: John Wiley & Sons, 1992.

_____ . *The Perfect Cover Letter*. New York: John Wiley & Sons, 1989.

_____ . *The Resume Kit*. Second Edition. New York: John Wiley & Sons, 1991.

Brennan, Lawrence D., et al. *Resumes for Better Jobs*. Fifth Edition. Toronto: Prentice-Hall Canada, 1991.

The Career Dictionary. 1994 Edition. Toronto: Encore Publishing Corporation, 1994.

Cordoza, Anne de Sola. *Winning Resumes for Computer Personnel*. Georgetown, Ont.: Barron's, 1994.

Eyler, David. *Resumes That Mean Business*. Revised Edition. New York: Random House, 1993.

Fry, Ron. *Your First Interview*. Second Edition. Hawthorne, N.J.: Career Press, 1993.

Hansen, Katherine, and Randall Hansen. *Dynamic Cover Letters*. Berkeley: Ten Speed Press, 1990.

Jackson, Tom. *Guerilla Tactics in the New Job Market*. Second Edition. New York: Bantam Books, 1991.

Kaplan, Robbie Miller. *Sure Hire Cover Letters*. New York: American Management Association, 1994.

Kent, George E. *You're Hired: Job Search Strategies for the 90s*. Toronto: Copp Clark Longman, 1994.

Krannich, Ronald, and Caryl Krannich. *Dynamite Cover Letters*. Woodbridge, Va.: Impact, 1991.

Lock, Robert P. *Student Activities for Career Planning*. Guide Book III. Monassas Park, Va.: Brooks/Cole Publishing, 1992.

Marcus, John J. *The Complete Job Interview Handbook*. Third Edition. New York: Harper Perennial, 1994.

Nadler, Burton Jay. *Naked at the Interview*. New York: John Wiley & Sons, 1994.

Resumes for College Students and Recent Graduates. Lincolnwood, Ill.: NTC, 1993.

Tepper, Ron. *Power Resumes*. Second Edition. New York: John Wiley & Sons, 1992.

Yate, Martin John. *Cover Letters That Knock 'Em Dead*. Holbrook, Mass.: Bob Adams, 1992.

_____ . *Knock 'Em Dead*. Holbrook, Mass.: Bob Adams, 1991.

_____ . *Resumes that Knock 'Em Dead*. Holbrook, Mass.: Bob Adams, 1988.

READER REPLY CARD

We are interested in your reaction to *Career Planning for Business: Profiles of Success* by Ted Goddard. You can help us to improve this book in future editions by completing this questionnaire.

1. What was your reason for using this book?
   - ❏ university course
   - ❏ continuing-education course
   - ❏ personal development
   - ❏ college course
   - ❏ professional
   - ❏ other interest _____

2. If you are a student, please identify your school and the course in which you used this book.

3. Which chapters or parts of this book did you use? Which did you omit?

4. What did you like best about this book? What did you like least?

5. Please identify any topics you think should be added to future editions.

6. Please add any comments or suggestions.

7. May we contact you for further information?

Name: _____

Address: _____

_____

_____

Phone: _____

(fold here and tape shut)

Heather McWhinney
Publisher, College Division
HARCOURT BRACE & COMPANY, CANADA
55 HORNER AVENUE
TORONTO, ONTARIO
M8Z 9Z9